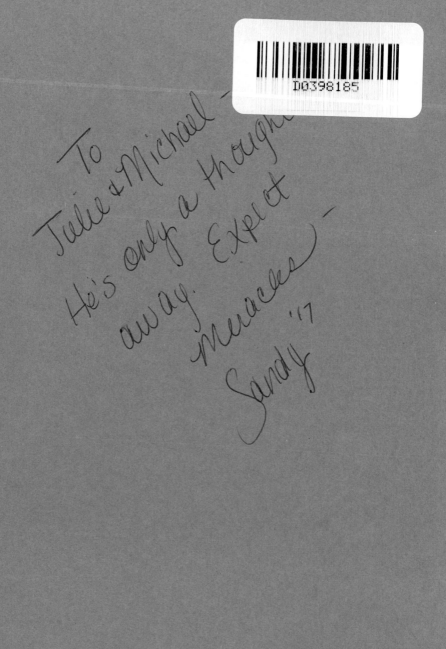

To
Julie & Michael –
He's only a thought
away. Expect
miracles –
Sandy
'17

LOVE NEVER DIES

JODERE
GROUP

Jodere Group, Inc.

San Diego, California

LOVE NEVER DIES

➤ **A Mother's Journey from Loss to Love**

Sandy Goodman

Published by: Jodere Group, Inc., P.O. Box 910147, San Diego, CA 92191-0147 • (800) 569-1002 • www.jodere.com

Design: Charles McStravick

CIP data available from the Library of Congress

ISBN 1-58872-015-2

04 03 02 01   4 3 2 1
1st printing, March 2002

Printed in Canada

To Mom,
who taught me how to be heard.
To Dad,
who taught me how to be still.
To Josh,
who taught me how to run free.
To Jeremy,
who taught me not to hide.
To Life,
that taught me to surrender.
To Love,
that taught me to persevere.
And to Death,
where I once again discovered all of the above.

— Jason

This book is dedicated to Love,
the source and the intention of all that is,
and to Jason who introduced me to Love.

— Sandy

Contents

Acknowledgments

I BELIEVE THAT WE ENTER INTO OUR PHYSICAL EXISTENCE with a "map" of the twists, turns, conditions, and relationships that will best facilitate our growth as spiritual beings. This blueprint we create, and our success in following it, centers on others who have agreed to accompany us. These "soul partners" will provide experiences designed to move us toward love. We would do well to remind ourselves often that each person we encounter either has a gift for us or is seeking one.

Based on this premise, I extend sincere gratitude to:

My husband of 28 years, for being my husband, my best friend, an incredible father to our children, and most important, my reason for sticking it out until the bitter end. I love you, Dave.

Jeremy, Jason, and Joshua, for choosing me as their mom and for proving the existence of unconditional love.

My parents, Ruth and J. Doyel, and my brother, Gary, for being my "first" family and for making that family abundant in joy, unfettered by fear.

Gladys, for loving my dad.

Becky Radford, for being the kind of friend every bereaved parent needs and for accepting the "new me" as if she'd known "her" forever.

Cyntha Craton, for sharing her passion for Spirit and giving me the courage to visit the most frightening place of all . . . the center of my being. This "Thank You" comes from there.

Barb Collins, for always listening, never quitting, and constantly questioning. Tenacity is contagious.

Stacey Doerr, for believing in me when I didn't believe in myself, and for allowing me to borrow from her huge cache of resilience and courage.

John Edward, for being the messenger, for providing the entire universe with renewed hope, and for kicking my butt out of *The Pit* and up to the rooftop.

Stephen Cooper, for being my sunshine on a cloudy day.

Debbie Luican, president of Jodere Group, for believing in me, in Jason, and in life.

My Compassionate Friends: Carol Yurick, Alice McLean, Sharon Bryant, Lisa Malek, Ellen Strube, Cheryl Cromb, and a multitude of others who are forever connected by our children in spirit. Thank you for carrying the torch and for showing me that I need not walk alone. . . .

Prologue

Love Never Dies

There is no end
To anything;
No separation,
No division.
We have confused illusion with reality.
Instead see this:
An unbroken circle of light,
Expanding,
Intensifying,
Until the illusion of separation
Ceases . . .
To . . .
Exist.

— Sandy, 2001

damn . . . awake again . . . cat must be gone . . . sirens
. . . it's hot . . . i wish jason would never have fed that
damn cat . . . its been yowling at our window for hours
. . . running away before i can even get close enough to
see it . . . jason needs to get home . . . he'll be exhausted
. . . they leave in twelve hours . . . exactly twelve hours
. . . he was so calm today considering how nervous he

must be feeling . . . weird . . . i can't believe they're going to be in the Navy . . . was that the phone . . . now what? another wrong number? some kid calling for one of the twins? so what if it's 2:30 in the morning . . . "hello" . . . "sandy, this is riverton pd . . . there's been some kind of electrical accident and jason was injured . . . you need to meet the ambulance at the hospital" . . . "okay, thank you" . . . *man, i wish he would learn how to time these scrapes and bumps so that they happen during office hours . . . now we'll have another emergency room bill . . .* "dave, get up. jason's been hurt or something, it's probably nothing, but we need to go to the hospital" . . . *fumbling in the dark, i find my clothes i had thrown on the floor and start dressing . . . dave asks what time it is and i tell him it's 2:45 . . . he throws his watch on the dresser and mumbles something about it being broke . . .* "it says it's five something instead of two" . . . *i go in and tell josh where we're going . . . he goes back to sleep . . . okay . . . he would have said something if jason were hurt bad . . . they're twins . . . he'd know . . . we arrive at one entrance to the hospital just as the ambulance pulls into the other . . . i can't walk toward the ambulance . . . my legs refuse . . . i go toward the main door . . . the one i have used countless other times for stitches and BB removals . . . dave stops at the back of the ambulance . . . as they wheel jason into the hospital they tell his dad how many volts of electricity have shot through our son . . . crying now, dave walks over to where i stand frozen . . . i force the words out . . .* "what's wrong? what did they say? what happened?" . . . *he tells me about the voltage . . . says it is impossible to*

*survive something that strong . . . i don't believe him . . .
i can hear jason talking in there . . . he sounds fine . . .
he sounds like he does when he has a migraine . . . he
must have bumped his head . . .* "are they sure he even
touched it? maybe something else touched the wire
. . . maybe he just hit his head . . . listen to him . . .
there's no way he could have been shocked and
sound like that . . . he's wide awake" *. . . we go into
the hallway outside of the room they have jason in . . .
i hear him calling* "mommy! daddy, daddy, daddy!"
*just like when his migraines are at their worst . . . now
i know he is okay . . . he is too coherent, he even got the
date and president right, i heard him . . . a doctor comes
out . . . i ask* "how is he?" *. . .* "if it were any worse,
he would be dead. i have never seen an electrical
shock this bad except a lady who was hit smack in
the middle of the forehead by lightning" *. . . there
is no air in this hallway . . .* "can we see him?" *. . .* "no
. . . not now . . . later." *. . . oh God please let him be okay,
don't let him die . . . let them be wrong . . . i can't take
this. . . please help us . . . help jason be okay . . . dave is
pacing the small waiting room reserved for emotionally
distraught family members . . . we go outside to smoke
. . . i reassure him . . .* "for it's gonna be okay . . . he
probably has a migraine from the fall . . . they don't
know what they're talking about . . . he'd be in a
coma if he'd really been shocked with that much
electricity . . . they're just guessing" *. . . please God
. . . please let him be okay . . . let this be just a horrible
mistake . . . please don't let him die . . . dave won't look
at me . . . he knows what I refuse to see . . . jason's friend*

who they have told us was with him comes into the hallway, an EMT holding her up . . . she is crying . . . we ask her what happened . . . "we climbed the building and on the way down jason just reached out and grabbed the wire that was by the fire escape and then he fell and hit the steps and he landed in the alley and he sat up and grabbed his arm and said 'whoa, what was that?' and then the police came and no we weren't drinking or anything" . . . *and she continues to cry . . . we go outside again . . . jason is now quiet . . . they come and tell us to go pack a bag and be ready to leave for salt lake city where jason will be transported as soon as life flight gets here . . . we ask again to see him . . . they say yes . . . for a minute . . . we go in . . . josh is with us now but i am not sure how he got here . . . we go into the room and jason is totally out . . . he has been given something to paralyze him . . . dave reaches up to smooth his hair back and the nurse squeezing the bag that sends air to my son's lungs says* "**Don't** touch him" . . . *dave jerks his hand back as if he's been burnt and i ask* "why" *and she mumbles something about not wanting him to move . . . as if he could . . . josh can't look at him . . . God, he looks dead . . . we go home and pack . . . we are back in fifteen minutes . . . maybe twenty . . . stacey and ken are here with us now . . . we sit in the waiting room and watch the clock . . . it's almost five thirty . . . the sun is coming up . . . oh God please let him live . . . don't let him die . . . he is our baby . . . i'm freezing in here . . . a doctor we know comes in and tells us he is strong and is doing good considering . . . he explains he is there to do surgery on his arm . . . to open it up* *because of the pressure building inside where the electricity burnt him and he talks about how electricity travels through muscle and that of course the heart is a muscle, but so far jason's heart is doing great . . . i start to breathe again and then he leaves and they are bringing jason back from doing a cat scan because he hit his head . . . someone yells and then they come and close the door and tell us not to leave for salt lake yet and i am paralyzed . . . my heart is pounding so loud i can't hear anything else . . . maybe if i don't hear it, it won't happen . . . please God . . . please do what is best for jason . . . whatever it is he needs . . . it is his needs . . . not ours . . . that matter . . . oh God, oh God, oh God . . . maybe if i block the door shut . . . yes, i'll find something to . . . it opens . . . it's the doctor . . . he's shaking his head . . . i close my eyes tight and concentrate . . . i won't listen . . . **i won't let him say it** . . .* "i'm sorry" . . . *i look up . . . heart pounding in my ears . . . i see his lips say,* "his heart stopped . . . we can't get him back . . . we tried" . . . *and the air is sucked out of the room . . .*

PART I

Losing

1
Preliminaries

Fragmented

"i'm sorry. . . ."
two words, so simple,
but when uttered by an emergency room doctor
in the gray of pre-dawn
they send a bolt of pain
> *through your heart*
> *that tears, rips, and punctures*
> *so brutally that*
> *no*
> *amount*
> *of time*
> > *will ever make*
> > > *that heart the same*
> > > > *again. . . .*

— Sandy, 1997

As I SIT TO BEGIN THIS BOOK, IT IS FOUR YEARS LATER, both a lifetime ago and only last week. Joshua, Jason's twin brother, is now 22, and Jeremy, our oldest son, is 26. Dave and I are entering our 28th year of marriage in rural Wyoming where we have lived since 1986. As we approach the anniversary of Jason's death, it seems destined that we share this story. Jason's death catapulted me into a search for truth that has expanded my view of reality tenfold.

It is important that you realize that this journey is mine. The experiences, obstacles, and conclusions are mine. Each of us progresses differently, and each event appears at the right place for that progression. Perhaps your choosing this book is one of those events. Perhaps it's not. I certainly do not know all the answers, and I believe that my truth is just that, mine.

I will write about grief, *as I experienced it.* If you lose or have lost a loved one, you may very well experience an entirely different process. However, my guess is that you will feel as if we have walked in the same shoes at least part of the way. I also want to spend some time talking about a few misconceptions about grief that are long overdue for extinction in our society.

When I share information about grief and all that goes with it, I apologize in advance for concentrating primarily on the death of a child. No matter how much revising I do, it continues to surface as the focal point.

I will write about my search for answers. Jason's death left a gaping hole in my life. I needed to fill that space with understanding. The fear that death might actually have the power it has been credited with held me hostage. I needed to know that Jason still lived, that the relationship we had shared was intact, and that love does not die.

And last, I will write about what I discovered along the path. I will recount the events that inspired me to begin this book—events that I hope will illuminate your soul and send you off on your own voyage of knowing.

I want to clarify that Jason's expertise in communicating from the other side has nothing to do with his level of spirituality before he passed. Jason was a very typical 18-year-old boy. He belched and passed gas, and the word *spiritual* was not in his vocabulary. He once left a church service prematurely because he thought the pastor was speaking in tongues . . . it was Spanish.

Neither is our persistent contact the result of an extraordinary bond of love between us. My heart is bursting with love for all three of my children. But on a scale of one to ten, Jason and I were smack in the middle at five, as average as any mother and son could be.

Jason began communicating with me because *I was relentless.* I begged, I pleaded, I bribed, and I did not stop. Before Jason died, if I wanted him or his brothers to clean their room or mow the lawn, I begged, I pleaded, and occasionally, I bribed. I even paid them a quarter an hour to behave on car trips. It worked. I continued with the same tactics after Jason passed.

Throughout the book, you will find bold, italicized segments that are my interpretations of Jason's thoughts on the subject. This is not channeled material or automatic writing. At least I don't anticipate it to be. It is simply a mom who knows her son well enough to feel comfortable putting words in his mouth. If he doesn't agree with what I think he'd write, he'll have to change it.

This is a book about life. It is about the passage from heartbreak to joy. It's about going beyond the obvious and seeing differently. It is my story and it is everyone's. If you take only one thing from it and claim it as your own, let it be this: Death is not an ending. Life is eternal. Love is immortal. There is no greater peace than finding that what you have feared the most does not exist, and there is no greater joy than knowing that love never leaves.

That's it in a nutshell. Eliminating fear, finding love. I couldn't have said it better if I'd said it myself. And just for the record, I did not pass gas or belch in public. . . .

2

Everything I Needed to Know...I Didn't Know

Silent Cries

There are times in my life when my heart
  cries out so loud for you
That I cringe,
Wondering what others might think
And then I realize
That only I can hear the screams.
They are a part of me,
Like the blood rushing through my veins
And the breath leaving my lungs.

—Sandy, 1996

W E HAVE NOT DONE WELL WITH DYING. WE HAVE denied its reality and considered it an end to life that should be avoided at all costs. We tell our children that Grandma died and went to a beautiful place called Heaven, and then we quit saying her name. We cart her clothes off to the Salvation Army, sell her house, cry (but only in secret) when someone inadvertently mentions her, and put all the pictures into storage. Instead of seeing death as the next stage of life and exploring the possibilities of such a belief, we choose to let fear keep us ignorant.

There are numerous presumptions about death and loss floating around in our society that need to be grounded. These fallacies about grief, adages meant to comfort, and suppositions passed down from one generation to the next, often do more harm than good. Those of us who have met death in person have a responsibility to introduce her to others and to share the reality of the emotional roller coaster she places us on.

Dr. Elisabeth Kübler-Ross has been credited with defining the five stages of grief as: Denial, Anger, Bargaining, Depression, and Acceptance. We've heard it from experts (who should know better) and from our well-meaning supporters. Unfortunately, what we've heard is wrong.

The doctor explained the concept in her landmark book, *On Death and Dying,* as the five steps an individual might move through upon learning of their terminal illness. She offered the stages when she wrote: "In the following pages is an attempt to summarize what we have learned from our dying patients in terms of coping mechanisms at the time of a terminal illness." During the 31 years since Dr. Kübler-Ross penned her now classic text, readers have somehow misconstrued the material and identified it as "The Five Stages of Grief." This was a grave (no pun) error on our part, but a superb illustration of our need to place death and dying in a neat little box that can be put away on a shelf and forgotten.

Reexamining my own experiences of grief, I can distinguish four areas I moved through to get from where I was to where I am. From the minute I comprehended the doctor's words and knew that my son was dead, until almost exactly six months later, I was numb. If you can imagine being emotionally anesthetized, that is the feeling . . . or lack of feeling. From that point until nearly two years later, I lived in a state of unyielding pain. The only thing that alleviated the pain was my hope that I could find proof of Jason's continued existence. I began searching for answers and used that search as a coping mechanism. As that search yielded results, and I changed my perception of both dying and living, I was able to start reinvesting in life and stop looking for shortcuts and hiding places. Therefore, if I were asked to list the phases I went through since Jason died, I would have to say:

- ➤ numbness
- ➤ unrelenting pain
- ➤ searching
- ➤ reinvestment

I am not implying that everyone could, should, or would take these same steps. There are many paths to choose from and a million forks in each path. No two people hurt exactly the same, for the same reasons, or for the same length of time. The pain of grief is as individual as a snowflake, and created minute by minute depending on where the griever is focused. The idea that there are specific steps to go through, in a defined sequence and for a definitive period of time, creates undue expectations not only for the griever, but also for their loved ones who anxiously await their "recovery."

. . . which brings up another fallacy. How many times have you or someone you've known asked, "Shouldn't they be back to normal by now?" Folks, we do not *recover* from the death of a loved one. Grief is not a disease. We do not "get well" from it. We begin at one point in our life, we go through what we need to go through, and we end at a *different* point in our life. We do not go back to where we started. Grief is a *normal* process that we go through when someone we love dies. We need to stop trying to make it *abnormal* and realize that each of us is going to confront it sooner or later.

My award for the most irrational platitude goes to whoever said, "Time heals all wounds." If I had my leg amputated tomorrow and I just sat and waited, would I stop wanting it a few months down the road? If you woke up tomorrow morning and found you were blind and you decided to go wait it out in the Caribbean, would you be feeling "back to your old self" in a year or two? Taking it further, would your co-workers expect you to be "over it" before the holiday celebrations began? Time heals nothing. Let me amend that. *Time by itself heals nothing.* Time is a bandage, designed to protect. It does not heal. Grief work begins on the inside and takes an enormous amount of energy and self-exploration. Even with tremendous support, the wound from a profound loss will remain as a scar that forever changes the bearer.

At a recent seminar in our community, a handout estimated that it takes approximately three to seven years after a loss (depending on the specific circumstances) for a bereaved person to reinvest in life. That is not three to seven years of hiding the hurt, stuffing the anger, and ignoring the guilt. That is three to seven years of confronting the numerous emotions that flood the senses before finally being able to embrace the loss and move through it.

When a loss is significant, we do not return to "our old selves." However, we should (and I despise "shoulds") find a way to be comfortable with our new self. I can remember a neighbor of ours coming to our house on the day that Jason died. He informed us that we would survive, and that he had survived the loss of two sons. He told us we would feel like we had basketballs lodged in our chests, and that although the basketballs would shrink in size over time, they would always be there. We have learned to feel comfortable with those basketballs right where they are. Said in total honesty, and meant to prepare us for what was ahead, those simple words stay firmly in my memory.

Others will expect the *"old you"* back. They will avoid mentioning your loss, they will suggest that you need to "get out and do something," and they will tell you it is time to get on with your life. *It is the only way they know how to react.* Many bereaved parents have told me that they've learned who their true friends are since losing their child. We become angry and distance ourselves from one friend after another.

We alienate ourselves from family members and say, "They don't care about me." And we quit. We quit family, we quit friends, we quit our jobs, and some of us quit life. It takes effort to share our pain with others. It takes effort to explain what we are feeling, when we are feeling it, and why we need others' support. It is much easier to simply end the relationship when it stops working and blame it all on their insensitivity. I say that's a cop-out. We need to be responsible. We cannot expect others to know our feelings if we guard them like treasures. Unfortunately, at the time I needed to share what I was feeling, I myself was critically lacking in knowledge of the entire grief process.

Many have asked me how they can help. What should they say? What is taboo? First of all, it is critical that you realize there is nothing, absolutely *no thing* that you or anyone can say to a parent who has lost a child that will make the pain go away. The pain is necessary. What others can do is show support by listening, listening again, and listening some more. There are also things to know, to say, to not say, and to do that will give a bereaved parent a sense of being understood. The following are common issues that are "normal" in the grieving process:

- ➤ fatigue
- ➤ memory loss
- ➤ daydreaming
- ➤ agitation

- ➤ inability to focus
- ➤ inability to finish tasks
- ➤ excessive sighing
- ➤ appearance of "doing better" and then slipping back
- ➤ tension
- ➤ magical thinking ("he will be back")
- ➤ suicidal thoughts
- ➤ crying at odd times
- ➤ blaming others
- ➤ irrational anger
- ➤ intense need to mention the child and what has happened
- ➤ depression
- ➤ guilt, shame, and anger
- ➤ intolerance of others' less significant problems
- ➤ lack of empathy

When you greet a parent whose child has died, instead of the usual "How are you?" (that we all know means "I don't really want to know but what else should I say?"), change it to "How are you *really* doing since _____ died?" We bereaved parents have an extreme desire to know that you remember that our child is dead. We want others to comprehend the magnitude of such a traumatic event. We want to hear our child's name over and over and over again. We want our bizarre behavior, our mood swings, and our forgetfulness to be pardoned. We think we're allowed, for as long as it takes.

We want to be able to talk about our child. We want to share memories of the time before their death and of the death itself, without someone changing the subject. Share stories with us about our children; tell us what you remember. And please share the happy memories. We want to be able to laugh without feeling guilty. Laughter, like tears, is wonderful healing energy.

We want acknowledgments on our child's birthday and death date, and we want to receive them forever. Don't mistakenly assume that the age of the child determines the impact of the loss. A child lost at zero days old is just as valuable to that mom and dad as a child who is sixty. Pain is pain.

Losing a child is not contagious. Don't avoid us. Don't be afraid to touch us; it can often be more comforting than words.

Don't ask us when we're going to be "over it" or how long you have to wait. We will never be who we were before. We have started over.

Don't try to find some reason for our child's death. There is no reason good enough.

Don't ask us how we feel if you don't want to hear, and please don't tell us you know how we feel. Unless we've told you, you don't know.

Losing a child has transformed me. I am not the same person I was four years ago. Before Jason's death, I had no idea who I was or why I was here. I had difficulty surviving a stressful day, let alone enduring the unthinkable. I existed, but I did not live. I had very little compassion and judged everyone and every situation as either good or bad. All of this has changed and will continue to change as I walk, and sometimes crawl, along this path I've chosen.

Do not misunderstand. I am certainly not grateful for my son's dying. I would give anything to turn back time and keep Jason home that night. But . . . my gratitude is immense for the well-marked trail I was led to and the light that has always appeared when blackness fell down around me.

Ya know, it's why we take a body . . . so that we can feel. If we'd all remember why we're there and especially remember we are just there for the blink of an eye, we'd hurt a lot less. But if everyone hurt a lot less, no one would need anyone else and the whole thing would be pointless. Go figure.

As far as Mom keeping me home that night, I was on my way out long before that day. I didn't really know it at the time, but looking back I can remember how easy it was for me to sign up for the Navy and how relaxed I felt. Mom remembers. I just signed up. Signed up for something I had no desire to do, didn't look back, was relaxed all the way through and even on the day before leaving. That wasn't me. If I had really felt like I was leaving the next day for months of push-ups, running, and "yes sir-ing," I would have been a total jerk to everyone. Instead, I was totally cool. When I walked away from my house and up the street that night, I felt like I was at the end of a long vacation. I'd had a great time, learned a lot of new things, and made some incredible friends. But I was tired and ready to go home.

So forget about your would haves, could haves, and should haves. When we're done doing what we go there to do, we're done. It's over whether the fat lady has sung or not.

Oh, one more thing. The light that Mom mentioned always appearing when she needed it? It was her own. We create what we need. Always. Remember that.

3
The Fog

Fantasy

Maybe if I concentrate hard enough
I can go back in time
And on the "night you left"
I can walk down the street with you
And when we get to the turn
That leads to the other side
I can make you stop before you go too far.

— Sandy, 1997

THE FIRST WEEK WAS A BLUR OF PEOPLE. I REMEMBER stumbling out of the hospital to the refuge of our truck, thinking that if we could just leave that building, the situation would change. I remember crying . . . and desperately wanting to leave, to go back to bed, to go back to Saturday, to go anywhere but where I was.

After signing various consent forms (consent for what, I don't know) in the parking lot, we drove home to find people already sitting in our living room. I recall being in the bathroom, the only safe place I could see. I pushed the door shut and sank to my knees. As I knelt there sobbing, the light went off for a few seconds and then came back on. Inadvertently, as if someone forced the corners of my mouth up into a curve, I smiled. My next memory is of calling Jeremy and telling him his brother had died. I do not recall the words I used, how he reacted, or how I dialed the phone. I do remember Jeremy saying that his fan, sitting next to his bed, had been going off and on for a couple of hours. Again, I smiled through the tears.

Friends and family propelled us through the motions of living. They told us when to eat, when to rest, when to talk on the phone and when not to. They hid the newspapers, turned off the local news, and basically sheltered us from things they felt we would find upsetting. They didn't know that we had already set up our own personal barriers from the outside world.

People were everywhere, and I only wanted to not be there. I needed to be with Jason, the Jason who had walked up the street the night before, not the one on a table at the funeral home. I wanted to go back to Sunday evening and forbid Jason's last night out with friends. I didn't want to choose between a cardboard casket and one that I wouldn't be able to pay for. I didn't want to ask the man in the suit if they had moderately priced ones and was grateful when our "experienced in funerals" friend whispered that the mid-priced ones were in the back room. I didn't want to hear an explanation of why pall bearers are a good thing. I didn't want to feel inspired when hundreds of balloons escorted Jason to another place. But I did it all. And at the end of the week, when other folks returned to their ordinary lives, a thick blanket of obscurity descended into ours. I called it *The Fog*. I welcomed it. I think I may have even created it.

I was not a stranger to death. My mom had died nearly five years earlier, and my only sibling had passed from cancer in 1993. In the early years of our marriage, Dave and I lost two babies in miscarriages, one of which required a memorial service. These losses were significant. Still, they did not prepare me for or compare to, the passing of my son.

I do not remember a great deal of the first six months. I was numb. *The Fog* was not only a barrier between me and the rest of the world, it permeated my entire being. I had to make lists of everything. My short-term memory had dissolved. My priorities changed. What had been meaningful was no longer significant, and what had not mattered before, became of utmost importance.

I shut off thoughts like turning off a radio. When my mind would drift into the night of his death and to Jason crying out for "mommy and daddy" from the emergency room, I would instantly summon *The Fog*. Although it had begun to lift periodically, I was adept at calling it back when reality tried to sneak into my consciousness.

Around Christmas and the twins' birthday, I began to worry that I was missing something by not allowing myself to feel. I was afraid that if too much time passed, the pain I had put aside might fade and take with it my memories and connection to Jason. The choking agony I felt when I allowed *The Fog* to recede was my only link to him. It was the absolute opposite of joy. And I began to crave it.

See? There it is. A need to feel pain. It's remembering why you're there. How can we know what joy feels like if we never feel the opposite? How will we learn how to comfort another if we haven't felt what they are feeling? It all works.

And about that morning, the morning I "lost my body." Hey . . . Mom always said I would lose my head if it wasn't attached. Jokes. Anyway, I was right there in the emergency room. I was hanging around, wondering what the heck I was going to do to get out of this one. It wasn't long before I realized that whatever I thought, I did. I thought of Josh, and there I was. I thought of Jeremy and zzzziiiippppp, right by his bed. I figured the fan out real fast. Then there was this tubelike thing with lights and colors and speed so fast I thought for sure I would disintegrate, and in what seemed like one split second I was in a beautiful field and Uncle Gary was tapping me on the shoulder. I remember thinking "Oh, shit! . . ." and realizing that this was a permanent condition, and then immediately recognizing the place I had "landed" while at the same time recalling the whole plan and . . . well, life goes on . . . literally.

4
Reality

Lesson

Losing you has taught me
That nothing is certain
And that in one split second
What we had assumed was the way things are
Never was.

— Sandy, 1997

ROUGHLY SIX MONTHS AFTER JASON DIED, I WOKE UP ONE morning to absolute clarity. Instead of *The Fog* I had grown so used to, I found clear, terrifying agony. Grief had arrived at my doorstep and I had let her in.

Someone told me once that we have a choice regarding the pain of grief. They explained that we can elect not to feel the intense sorrow and can choose other reactions to a loved one's death. Since I have always insisted that being with the pain is a necessary part of grieving, my first instinct was to argue the above statement. Something nagged at me, though, and I took a step back and pondered the conflicting idea.

After examining my own grief and discussing grief with others, I now concur with the above opinion *to a degree*. I believe that there are losses that for whatever reason do not hurl us into *The Pit*, that gut-wrenching place where all light is extinguished and pain is our only companion. I agree that we can *sometimes* choose to move past the pain of grief and get on with our lives. But we must be completely honest with ourselves in making that choice and must be sure to leave no stones unturned.

There is a powerful temptation to shift into "I just won't think about it and I'll be fine" mode. During the first few weeks, or even months, this approach works. It stops us from going beyond what we are ready and able to confront. I clearly remember shutting down when my mind wandered into intolerable territory. However, after the initial shock wears off and we return to the real world, untouched pain festers and swells beyond recognition. It doesn't disappear, lessen in intensity, or change into something else. It must be felt.

Therefore, here's my new theory on the necessity of visiting *The Pit*. I believe that we only need to be in *The Pit* if we find ourselves in it. If you are moving along and feeling sad but hopeful, and tired but capable, then you can probably move right along . . . until the next life-changing event knocks you to your knees. On the other hand, if you are afraid to look at your loved one's picture, unable to say their name, and avoiding your car because you can cry there, it's time to stop and feel. You have some work to do.

Before "grief work" can even begin, we have to be with the pain. The only way to do that is by going directly through the center. We have to be in *The Pit*. As deep and as dark and as cold as it is, we have to stay there long enough to want a way out. We cannot pretend it is not there or wait for it to disappear. We cannot take a short cut, walking around the edge and avoiding the inevitable. We cannot rise above it, or expect others to carry us. We must experience it until we begin seeing differently.

I walked to the edge of *The Pit* and descended as if I were going to a sanctuary. I settled into a corner of my own, found a blanket to keep me warm, and lit a candle to look into when the darkness became too great. And then I felt the pain. . . .

I went through nights so black I thought I would go mad. The pain slammed me to my knees when I least expected it, like a wave from the ocean hitting me from behind.

I chose not to fasten my seat belt, and I knowingly ignored stoplights before crossing a street.

I avoided thinking about Jason being dead, and played "let's pretend" for hours. I saw him walking down streets, sitting at stop lights, and shopping at Kmart. Sometimes I followed him, sure that a mistake had been made and that I would be the one to discover the error.

I found support and kindness from people I barely knew, while some of my closest friends were unable to meet my eyes.

I wanted to talk about Jason incessantly, but no one could endure listening.

I was consumed with what could have been and what should have been, and why it wasn't.

I refrained from going places where I had been with my son but spent hours in the alley where he fell.

Some mornings, I was unable to get out of bed. Some nights, I could not sleep.

I cried.

I screamed.

I isolated myself.

I surrounded myself with people.

It was the most excruciating pain I have ever experienced . . . until it became my salvation.

I had gone to the cemetery. I do not believe that Jason is any more in his grave than he is in Tahiti, but I relish the serenity of sitting by "his rock" and the unlikely chance of anyone stopping by to talk about the weather. On this particular day, I sat in the summer sunshine and considered why I was drawn there so often. I thought about a few days before when I had sat across the street and stared at the fire escape where Jason stood before grabbing the power line. It appeared as if I was craving the pain, but how could that be? I had felt nothing **but** pain for months now. *The Pit* was created for that purpose. Why would I yearn for more?

Unable to suppress the longing, I closed my eyes and called up the hospital imagery. Once again, I heard my son calling "Mommy . . . Daddy, Daddy, Daddy." This time I remained in the memory . . . and I cried. Sobs racked my body as I dug my fingernails into the new grass. As sorrow enveloped me, I became conscious of another emotion just on the edge of my awareness. Lurking in the shadows of my pain, awaiting my attention, was love. Waves of feeling washed over me, and while tears rolled down my face, I laughed out loud at the joy of it all. Those who have experienced this sensation, this "whooshing" of intense emotion, will know what I am speaking of.

There are many who do not want to feel better. They do not want to survive. They instead use their grief as they would a prized possession belonging to their loved one who has passed. They hold it close and keep it exactly as it is, wrongly thinking that changing it will change what it represents. All of us are there at some point. But once we choose to walk the path, we have to let go of all that holds us back. We do *not* have to let go of the one we've lost. We only have to let go of the fear and anger and guilt and shame that often accompany a loss. We have to make that conscious decision to get better. Once I understood that the polarity of the energy was shifting, while the strength remained the same, I was able to embrace the grief, release the fear, and look beyond the pain. I clambered out of *The Pit* that had been my home for nearly a year, shielded my eyes from the sun, and began my journey.

This was hard for me to watch. I wanted to show up in their bedroom and say "Look, here I am, alive, just different! Stop your sniveling!" But that would have defeated the whole purpose (and would have taken a lot of energy on my part). At any rate, it wasn't time. Mom had to perceive the loss before she could feel the need to look beyond it. And she knows me well enough to know that I never could handle bawling and emotional upheaval. When she cried, I stayed at arm's length.

There was one night I remember very clearly. Mom was sitting in the front yard of our house, in our neighbor's chair left there since "the funeral." She had my afghan and was getting it all wet and snotty with her crying. She looked up at the stars and said . . . well . . . screamed is more like it, "Give me something to hang onto! Let me know this isn't all there is! I need to know you're still here!!!" At the same time, I heard an almost identical plea from someone else, not far from Mom. I couldn't really tell where it was, we're short on atlases here, but this woman was seeking proof of something more and was doing the crying thing, too. I knew immediately that she was not a stranger. Her energy was familiar, and I knew she would "hear" me if I replied. But I remained silent. It was too soon.

The "whooshing" Mom described is pure unconditional love. You don't have to endure a huge loss or go through hell (which, by the way, is a human creation, not ours) to feel it. It's just that most folks in the physical don't take time to listen to their hearts. Once that heart is broken, they have no choice. It's wide open and screaming.

5
Searching

Clarity

Like traveling through a fog filled valley
My senses struggle to make sense of the blurred landmarks
I have grown used to.
Searching for a familiar turn,
the swirling mist gives way to clarity,
assaulting me with what I had feared most . . .
An unfamiliar landscape.
Fear replaces the blandness of not knowing
as ominous terrain beckons me forth.
Turning back to the luxury of ignorance
I find no fog behind me,
and realize that what I had felt familiar
was really only more of the black unknown.
Lost and alone,
I sink to the ground in surrender,
Mourning the loss of all I have known,
And seeing my first glint of light
in the tear
that falls
from my eye . . .

— Sandy, 2001

THE SEARCH I EMBARKED UPON WAS PARALLEL TO MY grieving, simultaneous but separate. I often felt like two people. One mourning and the other finding joy and comfort in the experiences triggered by the death of her child.

Initially, my search was focused on validating the reality of an afterlife. Beyond that, I wanted to know that Jason was still my son and would always be my son. I accepted the likelihood that he would grow into a more "evolved" being on the other side, but I needed desperately to know that the love between a mother and her child was eternal. Because I consider the love between a parent and child as the only truly unconditional love, there should be nothing, including death, capable of destroying it. I had to know that love endures, that Jason was still my son, that I was still his mother. If death was an end, just *poof* and we're outta here, gone from existence, then there could not possibly be a God. At least not one that fit my idea of God. And if there was no God and no afterlife, I wasn't hanging around.

I wanted to talk with others who had traveled the same road. I needed to share and compare and listen. I wanted to help when I could, and I wanted support when I was struggling. I joined grief mailing lists on the Internet. I found chat rooms where sharing was anonymous and safe. I read books not only about grief and child loss, but books about mediums, books about life after death, and books about God. Martin and Romanowski's *Our Children Forever* became my Bible. I soaked up information like a sponge. What felt right? What made sense?

As my exploration began to reap answers and my fears diminished, I soon realized that truth, my truth, anyway, would never be constant. It would change as I changed, flowing in and around the shadows of my life. Each day still brings new wisdom. As I began to feel the fulfillment of validation, I once again felt a tug to get moving. I knew then that this was not a journey with a defined "end" in sight.

The "feeling-like-two-people" thing is exactly right. I had to tiptoe in to visit, 'cuz I never knew if she would laugh, smile, cry, or have a heart attack. The moods and changes were crazy. This is about the time that Mom started talking to me constantly. It was her persistence that fueled my determination. Just as she said in the introduction, she was relentless. There were people who told her she would have to let go, that she couldn't continue, that she was "holding me back." As if she could. What a kick! What would happen if I was held back too long? I'd fall from the sky? I'd become alive again? Sheesh. Slow, vibrating souls say the darnest things. My mom's perseverance (bordering on come-hell-or-high water stubbornness) inspired me. I wanted to do as much as I could, as fast as I could. I knew there had to be a way to reach her. So while Mom searched, so did I. I found a treasure trove. And I am not even halfway through the goodies.

I learned how to "nudge" Mom in the right direction. I could hook into her energy and make her want a song from me when I knew one was coming on her radio. I could, and did, assist in directing her toward the right people to help her. I could, and did, introduce her to Ocallah and to John. I will talk about this more later if Mom doesn't, but let me just say that I was the one doing the manipulating on this item, not her. However, without her constant love and determination, I would not have known what was right for her soul development. She let me know every step along the way where she was going and why. So go ahead and be relentless, as long as you know where you're going and why. You have our permission.

I also want to mention that as she met more and more people on the Internet, I met more and more souls. And those I met were connected to those Mom met. It was like we were mirroring each other. Mom made a friend, and I made a friend who knew Mom's friend. Or maybe it was I met someone, and then Mom met someone who knew the someone I had met. Hmmm . . . oh well, it's all immaterial. And again, that's literally.

6
Reinvestment

Hope

When the sun sits down on the mountains
and the clouds turn purple and pink
and golden rays send fingers out to touch me,
I stop breathing and inhale with my heart
because I know
that along those glittering strands of light
lies my connection
to you.

— Sandy, 1997

WANT SOMETHING DONE? ASK A BEREAVED PARENT. WE will do anything in our child's name. A huge amount of energy goes into loving and raising a child. And then another wave of energy goes into grieving their death. As that starts to subside, *we need something to do.*

After rebuilding myself and reaching a point where I felt somewhat comfortable with the new me, I began wanting to make a difference. Dave and I had attended the National Compassionate Friends

(NCF) Conference in Philadelphia during the summer and had felt the positive impact of NCF's efforts. We formed a steering committee and chartered a local chapter in December of 1997. Bereaved parents began showing up at our meetings, and my need to make a difference was realized. One thing I learned very early in my grieving was the incredible healing power of helping others. NCF was my tool for doing that. When people thank me for listening or for some bit of wisdom I share, I actually feel guilty because I am selfishly helping myself by helping them.

After our NCF group was established (or maybe before, I don't really have dates down pat) we adopted a long, skinny piece of land from the city and began developing "Jason's Park." We chose a location on Main Street, where Jason spent a large percentage of his time; and others have brought memorial trees, plants, and benches in. After three growing seasons, we have eliminated about half of the weeds, built a wishing well, a swing, and a picnic table. Our NCF group sponsored the construction of a brick memorial wall in the summer of 2000. Nearly all parents who have lost a child will at one time or another worry about their child being forgotten. I remember the fear of no one knowing in ten or twenty years that Jason had even lived. Jason's Park has alleviated that fear.

I also write poetry. Each time I sit to compose a new verse, I am right there with Jason. It is my time for him. In my day-to-day life, I give time to Joshua, Jeremy, Dave, my employer and our clients, and to myself. My poems, my NCF work, and the upkeep at Jason's Park . . . all of that is Jason's time. I wish I could pass that time sharing a pop on the front porch, but we don't always get what we want. . . .

Finally, this book is for Jason. It is a celebration of life. I want desperately for it to touch others, creating a ladder of love for those who are futilely trying to claw their way out of *The Pit*, but even if that doesn't happen, I delight in simply sharing Jason's story.

I have made this appear as if reinvestment is all about *doing*, and that is not the case. Reinvesting in life is about feeling better. It is about finding a new place to fit, for the new person I am becoming. It is about celebrating Jason's existence, both here in the physical and here in the spiritual. I have done well preparing and maintaining "things" that remind those who knew Jason of his life before he crossed. I have a great deal of work to do toward sharing what I now know is his continued life after passing. It is difficult to disclose beliefs that are likely to raise eyebrows. However, I am much more complacent with that sharing now than I was in the beginning. Not talking about the afterlife and what I have experienced is no longer an option in my life. It is very much a part of me, a part that has sustained me. A part that has reminded me to breathe when I've been too tired to make the effort.

A word of warning here to those of you who have lost a child. Do not get so caught up in what you are doing that you forget to notice what you are feeling. Remember, the only way to the other side of it is through it.

This book. I've told her to write it. I made it impossible for her to resist. If it doesn't get to the right people, someone else will write another one that will. We are intent on sharing the light. It is up to you to decide whether you want to look into it or look away.

The NCF chapter has been and will continue to be wonderful. So much has happened there, so many friendships forged. The poems . . . you have them right here in this book. Was it therapeutic? You decide.

Jason's Park is another story. Quite frankly, I think my parents are nuts. They go down there in 100-degree heat to rake. Mom pulls 10 weeds out of 5,000, and Dad builds things to set up in The Park so he won't have to pull weeds. When they dedicated the first memorial wall and let the balloons go, my mom asked for my opinion on the wall. I came through to a medium on that very night with my genuine sentiment. "They've built the Great Wall of China." Like I said, they gotta be nuts.

PART II

Seeking

7

Groundwork

A Thought

You came into our lives,
 grabbed pieces of our hearts,
  and then left with them still clutched in your fist.
No time for goodbyes,
 no knowledge of your destination.
I think that maybe that is the way you wanted it . . .
Just "Bye, see ya later, I love you"
Instead of racking, screaming sorrow . . . that would have been.
 (Your tolerance for tears was never great . . .)
I wonder if maybe WE planned it this way . . . before . . .
To have this life
 . . . this loss
  . . . at this time
 so that we would have this stabbing pain—
 to know the joy of love . . .
 to have this gut wrenching jolt of death—
 to know the wonder of life.
Perhaps you only came to us, with us,
 so that we would see what we have
  instead of thinking that all we have is what we see.
Perhaps your purpose
 was only to lift the veil
  and force us to look at the light.
        — Sandy, 1998

EVERYTHING IN MY LIFE IS EITHER *BEFORE OR AFTER*. THERE is a distinct break in my reality that occurred when Jason died. I remember only bits and pieces of my life *before* that morning. It seems like another lifetime that I can vaguely recall, but not clearly or logically. *After?* Well, as I said before, there have been two "me's" existing during the past four years. One standing in the shadows and one in the light. I have introduced the first "me" to you already. I'd like to spend the rest of our time together talking about the "me" I am becoming.

From the very beginning, I was obsessed with finding my son. He had been taken from me in an undetermined condition and hidden in an unknown place. I had no way of reaching him, no clues to go on, and no one to assist me in my search. There are no private detectives who specialize in finding the souls of dead children. Friends and family members want us to move on, get over it, find closure. If we are lucky enough to have supporters who understand the trauma of a child's death, they seldom consider it healthy to obsess over a death when we have living loved ones to think about.

I did the only thing I felt capable of doing. I pretended to be "progressing" through the grief normally. I smiled when I knew it was expected of me, I stopped constantly talking about Jason, I was discreet when visiting the "new age" section of the bookstore, and I only discussed my new "hobby" with those who shared my interests. It appeared as if I were "accepting" Jason's death, when in reality I was hanging on to life by the tips of my fingers.

I started with books, discovered the Internet, found like-minded friends, and began meditating. I spent more time outside in soft, quiet places; and decreased the noise and chaos in my life. I began a workout program with a friend, inventoried my "beliefs," and began searching for a God I could embrace. Eventually, I dumped all the garbage I had labeled as truth. All of this served in opening my awareness to what could be. The more I believed, the more I experienced. The more I experienced, the closer I was to Jason. None of these actions are finished. They are, and will remain, works in progress.

I began by reading every book I could get my hands on that had the slightest likelihood of answering the question, "What happens next?" I read books by and about mediums. I read books about the afterlife. I read books about Buddhism, Christianity, Taoism, and Spiritualism. I perused texts on spirit guides, angels, and meditation. I studied channeling, astral travel, dream interpretation, and after-death communications (ADCs). Just as I began to fret that I had read every book in print that could aid me in my search, lo and behold, I discovered the Internet. Suddenly I had a library in my living room. I subscribed to grief and spirituality mailing lists and afterlife bulletin boards. I devoured hundreds of e-mails a day and was still starving for information.

Once I became proficient on the Internet, I attempted chatting and found the best of both worlds: knowledge, and real-life people to share with. Here were folks who grasped exactly what I was looking for. I met numerous individuals online who had lost children, and while some were just beginning their journey, others were far beyond me on the path. I found chat rooms for grief work, mediumship, after death communications, and chat rooms regarding spirituality in general. It seemed that the more knowledge I gathered, the larger the hole I was filling with that knowledge became.

I try to balance my time spent reading and being online with time alone and time appreciating nature. I crave peace and quiet and find that as I grow in awareness, my sensitivity to sound and confusion escalates. I used to be able to sit in a room with a highly charged movie playing on television and be capable of tuning it out. That is no longer possible. I use the tranquility of the cemetery and the stillness of candles to bring me to my own place of peace.

I also strive to put some sort of physical activity into my schedule. Everyone needs balance. When my health is slipping or my energy level is low, I can't maintain a high level of spiritual awareness. It simply isn't possible.

Since employment has to fit in here somewhere, this is not an easy agenda, but when I manage to squeeze it all in, the difference it makes in the energy I project is obvious. My outlook on life is more positive, my ability to listen to the silence is heightened, and I am more open to what comes my way instead of blocking it all out or not paying attention.

A few other things have been imperative to my search: meditation, correcting my perceptions, relinquishing fear-based ideas, and finding a God I like. Since these matters are going to require more than a page or two, I guess we're moving on to the next chapter.

Right there, at the end of this chapter, my mom had a fear-based belief that chapters in a book should be longer than a page or two. She also thinks books have to be at least 150 pages long. John told her not to worry ("You're not in school"), but she still doesn't get this writing thing (grin).

Books are good, the Web is good, anything that will expand your view of what is real (and what isn't) is good. When you go to the bookstore, watch for what catches your attention. If a book falls on your foot, make sure you look at it before calling the store owner a sloppy shopkeeper. Rule number one: There are no coincidences.

Nature . . . how much closer can you get to death than life itself?

Noise . . . or need to have less of it? It's only your soul wanting to hear itself. Honor that wish as often as you can.

Exercise. Mom asked me once if she was spending too much time on physical stuff and not enough on the spiritual, and if I remember correctly, I told her that they are one and the same. There is no separation between physical and nonphysical since one can't be there on Earth without the other. Well, I guess I could be there without the physical, but why would I want to? Here is there anyway, only here is there without all the crap and anything we want to replace it. Make sense? I also told her that it isn't what you are doing but where you are at when you're doing it. If you are coming from love, it's all spiritual.

Now, listen up. This is important. As you read your books and share in your chat rooms, you will encounter tons of information. All of it is someone else's truth. It is not yours unless you claim it as your own. Be discerning. Be mindful of how the information feels to you. If it doesn't feel right, ring true, yada yada, leave it there. Don't take it. It's not yours. This applies to everything you come across as you search for your answers. If it isn't a good fit, it wasn't meant to be yours. Okay?

8

Meditation

Surrender

Words elude me.
Drowning in feelings,
I sink to the center of my being,
briefly grasping the meaning
Inside is everything.
All that exists is there.
Assaulted by emotion
I flinch and turn to go
But hear a silent voice
Saying . . . "No . . . stay . . . ALLOW."
And so I do.

— Sandy, 2000

I AM PROBABLY THE LAST PERSON THAT SHOULD BE SAYING how, when, and where to meditate. I have set a goal of daily meditation at least a hundred times, and I haven't succeeded for more than three consecutive days. It isn't a matter of not *liking* to meditate. I do, I really do. It is a matter of not taking the time to do it. I need to make it a priority in my life, and as of today, I haven't. So as you read what I think you should do, please take it with a grain of salt.

First of all, some things to avoid:

➤ Don't try to force something to occur. If you go into a trance and see Jesus, Buddha, and Elvis, that's fantastic. But don't go into your meditation expecting it.

➤ Don't overevaluate the meditation. When it's over, enjoy the serenity and just be with it as it is. Analyzing takes away the feeling.

➤ Don't spend a lot of time trying to make your mind empty. You will experience a quieting of your mind, but it will happen spontaneously when you find the right meditation.

➤ Don't worry about "doing it right." Any attempt to listen to your heart is better than no attempt at all.

Now for the do's:

➤ Find a quiet place. No telephone, no television, no doorbell. If that means you have to take a pillow into the bathroom and lock the door, then do it. If the bathroom is a busy place at your home, I suggest you go to your local cemetery. Take a flower, sit by a grave, and don't make eye contact with anyone. I can almost guarantee you won't be bothered.

- ➤ Make sure you have gone to the bathroom and gotten a drink before you start. If you're hungry, have a snack.

- ➤ Get comfortable. Take off your shoes, loosen your clothing, relax. I cannot lay down without going to sleep, so I have to sit up. However, if you can stay awake, lying down is fine.

- ➤ Close your eyes and relax your body. Beginning at your feet and moving up to your head, tense and then relax every muscle group. Hold the tension and inhale, then relax as you exhale. Once you get the hang of this, you won't need to actually go through each step. A breath or two and you will automatically relax.

- ➤ Focus on your breathing. Breathe in through your nose, and out through your mouth. I am not sure why this works best, but it does. Make sure you take deep breaths, filling your lungs and stomach. Hold each breath as long as you can between the inhale and the exhale.

Okay, you're good to go. You can keep your eyes open if it works, or close them if it doesn't. I close mine and stare at the back of my eyelids. If I focus on that blackness, I can keep my thoughts at bay, which is what you want to eventually accomplish.

After many periods of watching that black wall, I was elated when it suddenly became three-dimensional. One minute I was looking at a flat surface, and the next minute I was in it. I felt like I could plunge into it, fly forever, and never touch physical matter. You will also see colors. Great splotches of iridescent colors, floating in from behind or approaching from in front of you. Just observe as you would a movie, and stay relaxed. Don't make the mistake of assuming that your meditation is complete if and when you stop seeing colors. Your meditation is complete when you choose to stop. Twenty to thirty minutes is good, and you'll most likely start feeling antsy by then. Just bring your awareness back to where you are and end your meditation.

There are numerous techniques for meditation. You might prefer listening to soothing music without vocals. There are tapes available that use a repeating tone (binaural beat) devised to shift your brain waves into specific states. Staring at a focal point and concentrating only on it can move some into a meditative state. It might be a blank space on a white wall, a pattern in a carpet, or a candle flame. Repeating a mantra (short phrase) either aloud or in your mind sometimes aids in reducing outside thoughts and noise. There are guided meditations that can be purchased on tape, or you can make your own by recording one in your own voice. Guided meditations take you through a relaxation process and usually some other type of "scene" where you are working toward a goal of centering, stress reduction, weight loss, etc. Try different methods until you find what works. Just before sliding over the edge into sleep, we pass through what is called a hypnogogic state. When I can hold on to that state of consciousness without moving on into actual sleep, I will almost always experience something nonphysical. It wasn't too long after I started meditating that while in this hypnogogic state I saw a very clear eye, lashes included. As it faded, I saw a sun, with a face, and the mouth was moving. I believe that was Jason's way of telling me to "Watch. Pay attention. Your son (sun) is talking to you." In another session, I hugged Jason and felt tears rolling down my face *here*, while feeling the joy of hugging him *there*.

Centering is meditation in action . . . staying in the calm. Being centered means not allowing your inner peace to be shattered by negative thoughts. When you are centered you are in a state of clarity and balance. A good centering technique will require only minimal concentration, permitting you to keep the majority of your attention on whatever else it is you are doing at the time. Here is an example of a very easy centering technique:

> ➤ Take several slow, deep breaths.

> ➤ With each in-breath, think or say "Breathe in calm."

> ➤ With each out-breath, think or say "Breathe out a smile." (It is nearly impossible to not smile when you do this.)

Meditating is not a way for me to directly and/or instantly link with Jason. It is a process that allows me to shake off the business of living in the physical. It erases the bills that are due tomorrow, the dishes that need to be washed, and the list on my desk. It brings me back to what matters, which is my center, which is love, which is what unites all of us. It reminds me of who I am. When I meditate regularly, I am much more open to what is going on beyond what I can see, hear, or touch. It's like a light switch in a dark room. Once you find it and learn how and when to use it, things become much clearer.

What the heck does "take it with a grain of salt" mean? Okay, Meditating 101. Sit. Relax. Breathe. Accept. That's it. No expectations, no rules. Do it regularly and you will never again be clueless as to what to do when feeling overwhelmed and anxious. I have been telling my mom for three years (of her time) that she has to meditate regularly if she wants to keep moving on this journey she's on. She ignores me. Go figure.

Will you be able to "see" the other side while meditating? Talk to passed loved ones? Hear their replies? Probably not. But consistent meditation expands your overall awareness so that more will be visible to you all of the time, rather than out of sight, out of mind.

9
Unpacking

Two Years

From the very first moment, I've known you would not be
coming back.
Still I wait.
When I hear the door open . . .
When I see your head bobbing above others in a crowd . . .
And when your scent fills the space around me . . .
I hold my breath.
I wait for that moment when sleep ends and I can celebrate . . .
"oh my, it was only a dream."
A nightmare of enormous proportions,
given as a gift to teach me of love,
remind me of wonder,
and fill me with compassion.
I wait endlessly . . .
But alas, there is no awakening, no revelation.
The horror is true.
It is but the wind at the door . . .
a stranger's bobbing head . . .
and someone else's scent, drifting in the breeze.
I am left with only a realization that even harsh reality . . .
can teach of love,
remind of wonder,
and fill with compassion.
A gift wrapped in barbed wire is as precious as one in tissue.
It is the anguish of finding the center that strengthens our souls.

— Sandy, 1998

SOMEWHERE BETWEEN SIX MONTHS AND A YEAR *AFTER*, I realized I was carrying around some extra baggage. So many of our beliefs are simply ideas that someone has shared and we have declared them ours. When confronted with a loss that rips us wide open, all of those beliefs are exposed and screaming for validation. It is then that we realize how much we have accepted merely to fill the empty space. In order to authenticate our own beliefs, we must first relabel them as "ideas." Beliefs are firm, rigid, and set in stone. Ideas are flexible. They can expand and twist and turn and disappear without leaving a trail of shame. So after absorbing information like a sponge, finding time to meditate, working out and spending time alone, I had to alter, add, and eliminate some ideas I had indiscriminately collected.

A perception is the way we see something. Before Jason died, I was comfortable concluding that death was the end of a life here on Earth, and that "something else" came after. I didn't buy into the orthodox heaven or hell theory, but I didn't think we just ceased to exist either. When Jason died, he took my ambiguity with him. I had to *know something* to put hope back into my life. I had to change my perception about death.

I think I have had assistance with this. As I question others about their convictions and experiences, I sometimes have bursts of insight. A dialogue will be going nowhere, and abruptly, an extraordinary concept will emerge. Occasionally, it's just a conversation in my head, a conglomeration of thoughts that suddenly click into place. Chills zip up my arm, and I immediately sense: *Pay attention.* These intuitive connections produce ideas that I can happily place in my "keep folder." I will relate some of these experiences later, but for now just be aware of the need to be flexible in what you believe.

Back to where I was *before*. I was born into a typical, two-children, father-works, mother-stays-home family. My parents did not discuss religion, and I do not recall ever having any kind of spiritual dialogue with them. I attended Sunday school, church, and vacation bible school, and was baptized at about twelve years of age. I "belonged" to the First Christian Church, and it must have been pretty low key since it failed to put the fear of God in me. When I hit high school and found other activities, religion took a back seat. Actually, I think it got out of the car entirely, because when Jason died, I was pretty empty in the faith department. I did believe in "something bigger than I was," but had no clue what that something was. I did know what it *wasn't*, and that is where I began.

What does faith have to do with any of this? I don't know how or if it fits into your journey, but I felt an inexorable push to explore and fill the empty spaces. It was inconceivable to me that we could live our lives and give all we have, only to have it yanked out from under us in one split second.

Relationships are a primary focus during our lives as physical beings. We spend nearly every waking hour either physically interacting in relationships or thinking about them. We establish them, nurture them, and invest our life in them, and then with one breath, it's over? No, it didn't feel right in my heart. I had to understand. Who created this? Whose idea was it? What is the rationale? If I could find the "writer" of this production we call life, perhaps I could know the conclusion. And then, possibly, I could trust that love doesn't just disappear, and I could find my son.

My mind would not tolerate a personalized God. The guy sitting in a big chair handing out judgments didn't cut it for me. My God had to be *all that is*. My God had to be energy and light and unconditional love. My God had to be not only around me, but inside of me, and not only inside of me, but inside of every single living thing. Finding that God in organized religion is unlikely. Finding that God anywhere outside of myself was impossible.

I had subscribed to a grief mailing list on the Internet. A mailing list is a group of individuals with a common interest who e-mail each other and the entire group. Usually, a note to one is a note to all. In this particular group, there were quite a few rather zealous, fundamentalist Christians. I would enter into their dialogues, and periodically someone would ask me what religion I was. Now I had always assumed, erroneously it appears, that being a kind person and trusting in a higher power qualified me as a Christian. So when queried, I would proudly and confidently reply, "Christian!" One day, I was sent the criteria in bulleted list form. I did not qualify.

Screeeech . . . ! Detour on the path. Suddenly, in addition to finding my own beliefs, I was responsible for informing others of what was wrong with theirs. On a mission, I became furious over statements such as "Don't worry, your son is sitting on Jesus' lap right now." How dare they tell me what my son was doing! Hearing that God needed him more than I did, or that God only took the best, infuriated me. No one, not even God, had the right to take my son. And, oh my, one statement as simple as "I will pray for you" could send me into a rage. I wanted the praying under my control, not theirs.

I became so judgmental of those who told me what to believe that I almost bypassed the "Dead End" sign on the side of the road. However, at the very last minute, my fury turned to indifference and then to empathy, and I realized that what had seemed to be a waste of time was an integral part of my growth. How could I believe in an accepting God when I myself had become judge, jury, and executioner to others?

Back on the journey, furiously reading new books and rereading old ones, logging onto Websites until the wee hours of the morning, praying to whomever might be listening, I searched for My God. I spent months researching different religions, talking to people who seemed to "know," visiting chat rooms, and joining more e-mail lists. No matter what I read, whom I talked to, or what I heard, I could not find the elusive answer. Not until I stopped to listen to myself did it suddenly become clear. The answer to my questions, the beliefs I needed to hold, were not something I would find in a book or on the Internet. The answer was the search itself. My God was within.

That is what searching is about. It is not about listening to the first person we talk to and agreeing with everything they say because we don't know where else to look. It is not about what our churches say, or our parents, or our Bible. It is about us. It is about going inside and listening to our hearts. It's sitting under a tree in the woods and hearing the wind whisper secrets in your ear. It's watching the sun set over the ocean and feeling as if you are a part of it. It's puppy kisses and your child sleeping and thunder that takes your breath away.

So the first thing I discovered about finding My God was to look within. I had to stop worrying about what everyone else wanted me to believe and start relying on myself. In a sense, I was fortunate to not have a huge stockpile of religious dogma to consider. I didn't have to clean house first. I only had to buy the appropriate furniture and set it in place, knowing of course that I might need to replace that furniture when new experiences changed my needs.

As My God became a concept that I could examine without bias, it was time to take inventory and lose any fear-based beliefs I had packed away. I do not believe that love and fear can exist in the same time and space. When fear is my guide, love isn't active. It may be present, but it's waiting patiently for its own turn.

My inventory was not lengthy. I do not believe in Satan, evil, or Hell. I cringe just capitalizing the words because they do not exist in my life. I do not believe that surrounding myself in white light is necessary. *Fear creates things to fear.* That's it. No more, no less. Now, if you feel a need to call for protection from your guides, or your God, or your guardian angel, by all means do so. But make sure that whatever you do has the desired effect of eliminating any fear you have lurking in the background. You can surround yourself with all the light in the universe, but if you're focused on fear, you'll create that which you fear.

For example, if I were to fear encountering evil spirits every time I closed my eyes to meditate, I would not be focused on love. My meditations would not be very calming. If I were to fear being unable to return to my body every time I try to go out of it, I would never leave (not that I have anyway). If I worried about running into Satan every time I talk to Jason, I would not be able to feel the love that is the conduit to our communications. I would not be where I am today. I would still be in *The Pit*. And *that* was hell.

Man. My mom used to get so caught up in those religious debates that she couldn't sleep at night. If it didn't fit into her agenda, she wanted it gone from the universe. But she softened. It was just a step she had to take to see how ridiculous it was. What does it matter where people get their strength? It all comes from the same source anyway. There is only one. Doesn't matter where you think it's coming from, as long as you know how to access it. And as long as you know that it's love. Love = God = Energy = All That Is = You = Me. One big happy family.

10

Perception Jolts

Now

There are moments
When I don't remember
Life before you left.
Like an insignificant dream
My past fades from lack of interest.
And even though THEN
is when you were HERE
I feel your presence
More intensely
In this moment
Now
Today.
Perhaps what I need to accept
is not your leaving,
but your becoming

— Sandy, 1999

E VER READ SOMETHING OR HAVE A THOUGHT POP INTO your head and all of a sudden every hair on your arm is standing up straight and the temperature in the room drops ten degrees? I call those flashes of insight *"ziiiiiiiiiiiings."* I am going to share a few of these episodes, realizing that they may have no impact on you. It was my beliefs that needed to be modified, and the reminders I received to do that may not be important in your journey. As you walk the path and pick up things along the way, you should *always* keep what feels good in your heart and leave the rest where you found it.

A perception held by every bereaved parent I know is that we long for our loved one's physical presence. When we are asked what hurts the most, we say "I miss his hugs." or "I miss seeing her." I said it. I believed it. Until I examined it and realized it wasn't true.

I was chatting with friends one evening when I was asked what it was like to lose a twin. The person who asked me was not a friend, but I had seen the nickname in the room a few times prior to that night.

"Sandy," she said, "what is it like to lose a twin? I mean, you have Josh and they *were* identical, weren't they?"

I was immediately seething. Just as I was ready to blast her with, "How could you be so stupid as to think one child could replace another!!" I felt Jason nudging me. He does that a lot. *Okay, fine,* I stopped and thought . . . *what is it **now**?* After a few minutes of pondering, I had my answer.

"Yes, Jason and Josh are identical twins," I typed, "and yes, if I really concentrate, I can *make Josh into Jason* when I am looking at him. I have, in fact, done that very thing a couple of times in the last month. However, I do not feel any solace or connection to Jason when I do it. I simply feel that I have made Josh look like Jason. That's it."

As often happens, I then private-messaged a friend to process what had just happened. I shared that this was certainly a cue to me to grasp that it is not Jason's physical body I miss. It is his presence. It is his energy. It is his spirit. If it was his body I missed, Joshua's would suffice.

I talked about when Jeremy is on his way home from New Mexico for Christmas. It is exciting and we can't wait to see him. We go to the airport and giddily wait for him to get off the plane. We hug, and we have a wonderful two-week visit. Do I hug him every waking moment? Do I sit and stare at him? Do I make him stay in the same room with me so that I can *see* him? No. I will get a hug before he leaves, and the interval is perfectly wonderful as it is *because his energy is nearby*. I can sense his presence. I know where he is. I know I can reach him.

When our perception switches from "It's his physical body I miss" to "I miss his presence," we take an enormous stride in our healing. We cannot bring back our loved one's physical form, but we *can* connect with their energy, their presence, with *who they are*.

Another inaccurate view I held was distinguishing love as separate from fear. I considered them to be two distinct emotions, existing apart. However, I was assisted in changing this perception, also. And again, I was online.

Chatting with a friend, she remarked that her ordeal of being molested as a toddler was similar to the loss of a child. Okay, at first I was piqued. If anyone but this wonderful woman had made such a statement, I would have come unglued. But this was a close friend who had helped me through some very dark nights. I couldn't react without thinking.

She went on to describe how she had found her "little girl self" in a guided meditation and had seen the energy as a gray mass. She recounted trying to touch it, and how difficult it was to make contact. It had sat untouched for over thirty years. I pondered that energy she described and speculated that it was the fear she had felt as a small child but couldn't comprehend, hence the putting it aside and separating herself from it.

I asked myself what energy I had "set aside" that I couldn't comprehend at the time of Jason's death? Easy answer. Fear. The same energy, the same feeling. Fear of Jason no longer existing, fear of my ability to survive, fear that I would *have* to survive.

During the months and years following Jason's passing, I was unable to ignore that cluster of energy that was conceived as fear. It was my steady companion, my security blanket, my candle in the dark. I cradled it in my arms as a way to link to Jason. I cared for it, I nourished it, I sustained it. And with that nurturing, the fear changed. It shifted from the negative aspect of the emotion, fear, to the positive one, love. The intensity of the energy did not change, only the polarity. As mentioned earlier, I recognized it when I sat at Jason's Rock that day. And here was the idea again, nose to nose with me, waiting to be acknowledged.

"Yes," I typed to my friend. "You're right. It is the same."

And then there are the insights that seem to come from some unknown source. We're writing a list of things we need to do and a poem comes out of nowhere. We are asked a question and an answer flies from our mouth. They're the things that are immediately followed by the thought: *Where did that come from?* Here's an example:

A friend, who is a medium, asked me, "Sandy, are you bothered by Jason coming to me so often? I mean, after all, he is *yours*." Pause.

"No, it's okay." I answered. "He's not *mine*. Actually . . . he never really was."

Okay, so why does any of this matter? It might not to you. It is meaningful to me because it is what helped me see differently. These were revelations for me. These three separate events erased three fear-based "ideas" I had. One, that I would never get to "see" Jason again and feel his closeness. Two, that the grief and pain would always be hanging over me and never change. And three, that Jason would no longer be "my" son. These lessons influenced me greatly, and I knew when they occurred that they were meant to be heeded.

Why do we persist in holding on to old perceptions? For instance, I have been in contact with Jason either through mediums or by myself for over three years. I still find myself reasoning, after a message, "She could have guessed that" or "I'm just making it up in my head." *Why* do I insist on vacillating over the easiest belief to live with? I mean, what are my options? I can postulate that Jason ceased to exist, is in the ground decaying, and I will never see him again. Or perhaps he is in hell, since he had not been baptized or accepted Jesus Christ as his personal savior. Or maybe he is in heaven and unable to contact his family because to do so would be a sin. Or I can accept that he is still with us, in a different form, just as he was still with us in a different form when he grew from infancy to school age to young adult. Choosing one of these four ideas is not a complex decision. But still, after all of the experiences I have had that validate the existence of an accessible afterlife, I continue to analyze and yearn for absolute proof.

Another analogy. I chat on the Internet with friends I have not physically met. I could, if skeptical of Internet communications, doubt the reality of their presence. I could, if I were raised to believe so, assume that those typing the messages are merely employees of the service providers, trained to be "friends" to the millions out there looking for someone to care. I could, if I had never chatted in a chat room, be clueless as to what chatting is about, and not really care. Those are some of the coulds. They are possible perceptions.

However, because of my experiences as I sit at my computer and type my messages, I *feel* my virtual friends around me. We share laughter and smiles, tears and disappointments, nonsense and wisdom. It never enters my mind to consider whether they are really who and what they say they are. They are right there, in the room with me. I can feel their presence, I care about them, I *know them*. If two Carols enter a chat room, I can *feel* which one is my friend from Philly. If someone is depressed and having a rough time of it, I can *feel* the sadness in their energy.

If we can feel the energy of individuals in a chat room when we picture them in our minds and talk with them, why can't we feel the energy of individuals who have passed on? Can't we envision them in our minds and talk with them? Why are we so quick to label it irrational? Why are we so hesitant to believe in the obvious?

Perhaps we hang on to inaccurate perceptions to justify our feelings. If a loss leaves us devastated, we have to hold a belief about that loss that justifies feeling devastated. If we are blaming others for a death, we have to view death as insufferable in order to excuse our vindictiveness. It is difficult to rationalize gut-wrenching pain if we absolutely believe in an afterlife that is full of joy and accessible to us in our physical lifetime.

So what's my defense? I am no longer devastated; the grief only surfaces occasionally. I am not blaming anyone for Jason's dying. My logic is simple. As long as I continue to doubt myself and long for that perfect validation, I can persist in searching. If I find my proof, 100 percent truth, I will no longer have the need to look, and find, and celebrate. Maybe hanging on to a bit of our old selves isn't such a bad thing. It certainly keeps me moving down the path.

Mom has some really good points here. The doubt will disappear when the time is right. She will come to a place in the journey when she doesn't need that as a motivator anymore.

There is one story she forgot to tell, so please allow me. About three years after I died, a local kid killed himself. She got the info via her compassionate friends' "line of communication" and immediately found herself needing to go to the cemetery to chat with me.

She sat by my rock, and after pulling a couple of weeds and cleaning some bird doo-doo off my picture, she blurted, "Thank you, Jason. Thank you for leaving in the way you did, and for being the way you are. You have given me a thousand gifts by dying."

Just as I thought "All right, Mom!" I heard her think, Oh . . . My . . . God!! Where did that come from, how could I say that, what was I thinking???!!!

Messages to you from us come in many ways. One way is by almost moving your own thoughts around to where they need to be. It's like interrupting a conversation to change its direction, only we're interrupting thoughts. After thinking about what she had said, and getting past the initial shock, she realized it was another step toward healing. Recognizing gifts in catastrophic events is not wrong. It is the first step in remembering who you are.

PART III

Discovering

11
After-Death Communications (ADCs)

Certainty

Last night,
in the glow of freshly fallen snow,
I felt for the first time in months,
. . . a sense of peace.
A feeling of wonder overcame me
and I looked around to see if you were there.
Later, I thought to myself,
"Why did I need to look?"
I know, as sure as I know how to breathe,
that you are with me always.
You are closer to me now than ever before
and the only difference is that instead
of opening my eyes to see you,
. . . now I must open my heart.

— Sandy, 1997

ORGANIZING THIS BOOK AS I AM, I MAY BE GIVING THE impression that everything happened chronologically. Death, grief, searching . . . one, two, three. . . . Bim, bang, boom. . . . That is not the case. The pain I felt, the searching, and Jason's contact with me all took place, and continues to evolve, concurrently. As I become emotionally stronger, Jason's energy seems to intensify. Or perhaps I become more receptive to contact as my emotions level out.

Anyway, as I begin this chapter, I find it necessary to . . . go back to the beginning.

Researched and named by Bill and Judy Guggenheim, an after-death communication (ADC) is explained on their Website as "an experience that occurs when you are contacted directly and spontaneously by a deceased family member or friend, without the use of psychics, mediums, rituals, or devices." The ADC Project originated in 1988 as the first complex research of after-death communications. The Guggenheims interviewed 2,000 people representing diverse religious, social, economic, educational, and occupational circumstances. They gathered more than 3,300 firsthand accounts from people who believe they have been contacted by a loved one who has died. Many of these reports can be read in their book, *Hello From Heaven*.

Contact from the other side can come to us in numerous forms. Electrical glitches, battery-operated devices switching off or on, items being moved from one spot to another, scents developing without a known source, temperature fluctuations, visual or auditory experiences, dream visitations and direct one-to-one communications are all portrayed in the Guggenheims' research.

We believe our first ADCs from Jason occurred on the morning he died, when the light went off and on in our bathroom and Jeremy's fan went off and on several times. Actually, that may not be entirely true. Something uncanny happened before that.

After being summoned to the hospital on the night this story began, we were dressing hurriedly when Dave asked me what time it was. I checked my watch and told him it was "two-forty-something." He held the watch up to his ear and then tossed it up on the dresser in frustration. "My watch is broken. It says it's *five-thirty-something*, and it's not running." The next day, when Dave checked his watch again, it was not only functioning, as in tick . . . tick . . . tick, but was displaying the correct time. Jason died at *five-thirty-something*.

I am not sure what this event meant. I do know that there are no coincidences.

Over the years since Jason's passing, we have had ADCs so frequently we see them now as commonplace. We say "Thanks, Jazz" and get on with our day. If we believe in an afterlife, why would we search for a physical explanation to, say, the television turning itself on? Would a service charge at the local electronics store be preferable to believing that your dad has stopped by to say hello? Again, we are afraid to think outside of the box.

I know a woman who is raising a beautiful little girl in an atmosphere where death is thought of as simply a change to another form of being. One afternoon, the lights were flickering, pulsing, and just being generally weird. The young girl, thinking out of the box as most children do, walked into the kitchen and heard her mom ask, "Did you see the lights just now?" The daughter looked up at the lights, not missing a stride, and said, "Yep, but don't worry. It's just a spirit."

I want to share some of the "signs" we feel we have received from Jason. I anticipate that some of you will not believe these to be actual after-death communications, and that's okay. What makes an ADC so validating to the receiver is the feeling of warmth and love that washes over us when one occurs. If you are desiring a contact from someone on the other side, don't spend your time *thinking about* possible smells, electrical glitches, or slamming doors. Instead, stop and let yourself *feel*. I think you'll be surprised at the results.

Jason was buried after graveside services on a warm July morning. We released balloons at the end of the ceremony as escorts for Jason as he began his journey home. Stacey, a very close friend who was with us every minute of those first horrifying days, was in charge of passing the balloons out to those who had come to tell Jason good-bye. When the service began, Stacey had the strings of our four balloons wrapped firmly around her hand. At the appropriate time, when she started our way to deliver our balloons, she was surprised to see that one had vanished. When she later related this story to me, she said "When I looked up and saw only three balloons, I thought, *He would do this. This is just like Jason to steal a balloon from me.*"

Becky, another very close friend from our hometown in Iowa, was with us through the first week of Jason's passing. When I think back to that day when she walked through our front door, I am belatedly astounded that she was able to put her life on hold, organize her home business for the time away, find her way through two huge airports, and fly nearly 1,000 miles. I only knew that she was with us, and that I needed her with us. So thank you, Becky. I now realize what a day that must have been for you.

Moving along, Becky manages a daycare center out of her home. Soon after returning from her trip to Wyoming, Becky was in her yard watching the numerous preschoolers in her care. In a brief moment of silence, she was startled by the sudden lights and bells of a toy fire truck sitting alone and untouched. The truck's light and bell had not worked before that moment, even when someone tried to trigger it. On another day soon after that one, Becky sat alone on her deck pondering the recent death of a sister-in-law, which triggered thoughts of Jason. A beautiful clear day was beginning to unfold, and Becky was surprised by the raindrops that began to fall from a cloudless sky. I know Becky well enough to know that she breathed a thanks into the void and smiled at whoever it was that was reminding her that love never leaves.

On a warm evening in September of that first year *after*, Dave and I had ridden our bikes along a pathway through our small town and had stopped to rest on Main Street. Dueling stereos, whistles, and roaring exhaust systems filled the night as carloads of kids sped past our solitary bench. We were three blocks from the building that Jason fell from, and although neither of us mentioned its ominous presence, we were oblivious to the activity and lost in *The Fog* while sitting less than four feet from the Saturday night traffic.

Suddenly, Dave broke our silent vigil by asking incredulously, "Where did these come from?" I glanced in his direction and saw that he was waving his arms around him as if he were being swarmed by bees.

Now, allow me to explain here that the balloons I mentioned earlier that were released at Jason's services carried thoughts of love. *After*, when I went to sit by Jason's Rock, I often blew bubbles (balloons are weather sensitive), sending them off with reflections of love. It became a ritual, and a bottle of bubbles sits at Jason's gravesite year round.

Totally baffled by Dave's swatting at thin air, I asked, "What? Where did *what* come from?"

"Can't you see them? Look at this! They're everywhere!"

Again, I asked "*What* is everywhere?"

"Bubbles . . . ," he said. "There are bubbles all around us."

There were no bubbles visible to me, but I am absolutely certain they were very real to Dave. The look of awe on his face as he stood there batting at the air did not ensue from an unseen or disbelieved origin. Jason sent his dad bubbles. And I am certain they carried thoughts of love.

On another autumn night, I stood in the yard of the group home where we lived and worked and watched the leaves on a lofty tree flutter wildly for over thirty minutes. There was absolutely no breeze, and nearby trees were motionless. I was so fascinated that I called Dave out to look. He had no explanation for the phenomenon, but likened it to a tree full of butterflies, fluttering their wings in delight.

It was also during the first fall that Josh called me at work and asked me to listen to a message on the answering machine. Now, as much as I hate saying this, the voice itself can only be described as eerie. It didn't sound male or female, and it was irregular in tone and volume. The message itself was routine. "Hello. This is Cindy. I was just calling to talk to Josh. I'll call back."

Now you need to remember that Jason and Josh are twins. Anything they could do to each other to cause discord was done. For at least the past year, Jason had called Josh "Susie Q," and Josh had called Jason "Cindy Sue." There was never a follow-up call.

Time gets a bit foggy for me here, but I believe that it was late in the first winter *after*, when Jason came to validate an earlier message he had given us. When you read about Lynn's mediumship reading in the next chapter, you'll understand my reference to validation.

It was a snowy afternoon and I had taken advantage of an empty house by lying down for a nap. I had been asleep for less than thirty minutes when I was awakened by the bang of the bedroom door slamming shut. Since there were no windows open to create a draft, and all pets were sleeping in the room with me, I got up to investigate. As I entered the living room and noticed the smoke from a candle that had obviously just been "blown" out, I immediately knew that Jason had decided to validate the message from nearly six months before. Again, I thanked him, and went back to my nap.

During these first few months, I remained ambiguous. I struggled constantly with confirming my son's existence on the other side while at the same time wanting him back. I was in *The Fog* and spending all of my energy on survival. I noted the signs from Jason and filed them away for another day. The only thing that would have eased the pain at that time was if someone had walked in our front door with Jason in tow, explaining with great embarrassment that a mistake had been made.

The first spring after Jason died, a beautiful purple flower grew in the middle of a row of yellow irises. I have been unable to identify the flower, and it has not grown there since. Hollyhocks that were white last year have bloomed purple this summer. This week, as I am writing this paragraph, another so-far unidentified purple flower has sprouted in our backyard garden.

This year on Mother's Day, I was sitting at my computer when I was flooded with the scent of flowers. I searched for the source to no avail. An hour later, I entered a chat room and was immediately sent a private message by Micki, a medium I had recently met.

"Did you get flowers for Mother's Day?" she asked.

"Nope, why?"

"Well, as soon as your nick showed up on my screen, Jason popped in and showed me a bouquet of multicolored flowers," she replied.

"Oh. Hmmm . . . maybe he was just giving them to me now."

I thought no more of it until I went to bed. Five minutes after falling asleep, I woke up with a start, a thought throbbing in my head. *The flowers Jason had that Micki saw . . . that was what I smelled.* It was my Mother's Day gift.

Just this past week, I went to trim around the roses at Jason's Rock. While there, I talked to him and told him I needed a sign. It had been about three weeks, which seems to be my limit. I also told him that if it was going to be a song on the radio (he is very good at this), to make it one that depicted him talking to me rather than my talking to him.

On the way home, I began smelling the same overwhelming scent of flowers. It became stronger and thicker and lasted as long as it took me to drive about a mile. Just as the scent disappeared, a song came on the radio that I often listen to when missing Jason, but one that I had never interpreted as a message from him to me. The song was Garth Brooks's *When You Come Back to Me Again*, and when I heard the lyrics, I knew Jason had heard my plea loud and clear, answering me with "In a song . . . I'm reaching out 'til we reach the circle's end."

After crying through that one and telling Jason thank you, another song had already commenced. This one was Jason's favorite "getting crazy" song, Mr. Brooks's *Friends in Low Places*, and of course it made me smile.

Jason has tossed our television remote from the buffet to the floor five feet away, and has left us dimes in peculiar locations. I found one in the bathtub, Jeremy found one in his sandal the day after I explained about Jason sending dimes, and Dave has found them on the armrest at the shooting range and in a clearing where he camped in the middle of a mountain range. Jason has turned on water faucets, flipped through channels on both our television and the radio in our vehicle, and rocked an unoccupied chair. These are the little things. These are the things that made us think "hmmmm" and then wonder if it really *is* him. However, I decided early in my journey that whenever there was the slightest chance of Jason being involved in an event, I would tell him thank you. Better to err on the side that feels good than to miss an opportunity to acknowledge my child.

Dreams

Many people ask how to differentiate a dream visit from a normal dream. If you've had a visit from a loved one while in a dream state, you'll have no need to ask that question. A difference in colors, the intensity, an ability to remember every minute detail forever, and a profound emotional impact are all present in a visit from the other side. Can we invoke a dream communication? Yes. How? Ask . . . and ask and ask. Each thought you send out into the universe finds its place.

A few weeks after Jason's crossing, his older brother, Jeremy, had a dream in which Jason appeared. Jeremy explained it to me the next day (and Jeremy is a man of few words) as follows:

"I was dreaming, and all of sudden Jason was there. I asked him 'Are you really here or is this just a dream?' He said, 'It's real,' and then I woke up."

My first dream visitation also occurred during the first few weeks. I was drifting off to sleep when an image popped up on my "screen." It was much like a snapshot, but with a line dividing the right half from the left. The right side was completely black like a negative. The left side was a full-length image of Jason, dressed in a tux, and eating something from a bag that I "felt" was popcorn. Now, even though it looked like a photograph, Jason was moving. There was no sound, no message, just a feeling of "See? Here I am." I was so stunned to suddenly see him and to *know* that he was really *there*, I woke up immediately, heart pounding like a bass drum. This is a perfect illustration of fear hindering the process, since even though I thanked him profusely, I am sure my emotional reaction was the basis of him waiting over three years before he tried it again.

While parents grieve the death of a child, they each enter their own little world of pain. Fear of hurting the other more than they already are hurt makes it difficult to share feelings and concerns.

Toward the end of November, Dave woke me up one morning to relate a dream he had just experienced. Before Dave could describe this dream to me, he was forced to disclose his recent thoughts of ending the horrifying pain he was in by suicide.

Dave had gone to bed the night before with that on his mind and had been visited by Jason during a night of deep sleep that in itself was unusual enough. Dave slept very little and very lightly, often getting up to work on projects that kept his mind occupied and his heart from aching. On this night, however, he fell asleep quickly. Jason came to him in the dream and took him by the hand. They went to a place that Dave could only describe as purple mist. He said it was a purple he had never seen before, both in its luminosity and its vibrancy. Jason sent Dave into the mist where Dave remembers listening to someone or something talk about his life here with me, Jeremy, and Joshua. He then remembers coming out of the mist, coming "back" to this reality with Jason and waking up. Waking up to a place in his heart where he had no desire to kill himself. Once again, Jason had sent his dad love.

Move ahead to Christmas, 1999. I had been asking Jason to show himself, to "appear," to "let me *see you!*" for about three months. I rationalized that it was the one thing that would convince me of his "realness." In one of those dialogues, I envisioned him promising that I would see him before Christmas. Sure enough, only a few days before the twenty-fifth, I had another dream visit. I was sleeping soundly this time. Jason sauntered into an unfamiliar room where Josh and I waited. He was grinning that cat-that-ate the-canary grin, and he was drinking a soda. I ran to him and hugged him, and then I led him over to a metal table and asked him to lie down. He looked at me strangely, but jumped up on the table and laid back. I slowly pinched and prodded his feet, kneecaps, arms, and face, apparently looking for my proof that he was real. I was so excited to finally *know*, and Jason put up with my silliness even though he was shaking his head in exasperation the whole time.

Mom has covered this pretty well. I have a couple things I want to add, though, since I am the expert on this subject. Another way we can connect to you is by entering your energy field and changing the way it feels to you. This might be felt as a chill or a "hairs on the back of my neck standing up" feeling. We can also send you thoughts, things that will just pop into your mind at odd times and you know as soon as you think it that you didn't think it (grin). Mom actually did talk about some of her experiences with this sort of thing back a couple of chapters, but it's always good to hear it straight from the horse's mouth.

We can create situations for you to learn from, and we can manipulate energy in ways that will affect the behavior of pets and animals around you. No, we don't "turn into" or reincarnate as animals. But we can enter their field of energy just as we do yours. So when the independent tomcat of yesterday crawls onto your lap to get a hug and a kiss, don't worry. We are quiet creative over here. . . .

. . . Which brings us to . . . the rest of the story (move over, Paul). We dead folks are not the only ones who can do the things you've just read about. All of us can. Me, you, your friend, your enemy, everyone. The way I see it, each of us has, nope, excuse me, each of us is, a piece of a soul (clump of energy, higher self, whatever name you want to give it). I think of it like a spark of energy that belongs to a larger mass of the same energy. I, the spark that is Jason, have no body containing or limiting me. No ego. I only have to think it (and sometimes this does take a little planning and scheming) and I can create it. The spark that is you can do the same with a little more work (and a lot slower). But only if you believe you can. First you have to know it, then you will experience it. Amen.

12

Mediumship

Freefall

Just as the sunlight moves particles of dust
From their stationary positions
So does love move us
Swirling
Falling
Rising
Sparkling.
We catch your warmth and join others
In our free fall.
The only decision we must make
Is whether to let the heat take us to unknown spaces
Or to cling with fear
To the first surface we touch.

— Sandy, 2000

MEDIUMSHIP IS THE ABILITY TO SENSE AND CONVEY communications from those who have died. A medium is an individual who has that ability. Information comes from spirit and is received by mediums in several unique ways:

➤ *Clairvoyance* means "clear vision" or "clear seeing." A clairvoyant is able to see objects, symbols, images, and scenes. For example, a spirit might show a medium what they looked like before they passed or show them a scene from a past Christmas or birthday celebration. Spirits show words, family names, and locations to validate that they are, in fact, communicating with the medium.

➤ *Clairaudient* means "clear hearing." A clairaudient is able to hear sounds and voices in their mind.

➤ *Clairsentience* is feeling a spirit's message. A spirit might convey emotions as to how they felt in life to validate their presence. They sometimes impart physical sensations to identify how they passed.

➤ *Clairalience* is "clear smelling," and clairambience is "clear tasting." A medium might smell a spirit's favorite perfume, taste or smell tobacco usage, or smell smoke from a fire.

None of this is simple to do, but I believe it is an ability that we all possess. Some are born with this capability already developed and some have to work at it. Since I am obviously of the second group, I have diligently searched for and successfully found several gifted mediums during the past four years.

There are those who might ask why "we" (in this case "we" means those grieving the death of a loved one) spend so much time searching for and observing mediums at work. The answer seems obvious to me, but I will explain it here just in case it's only obvious to those who have experienced "mediumship dependence."

As I've explained, when Jason died, I did not lose my need to hear from him. In fact, the fear that he might be totally gone from my life increased that need. When I found Internet sites, books, or television shows that validated mediumship, it was like finding a telephone that Jason could call me on. If I was there, in the right place at the right time, he would call. It's a simple explanation for a complicated situation, but it works.

Because of our programming regarding death and an afterlife, we demand a lot of our mediums. We want names and dates and whistles and bells. In a perfect world, Jason would have come through in our very first reading with: *"Jason Cole Goodman here, Social Security number 555-55-5555, hair blond, eyes blue, born in Council Bluffs, Iowa, at Mercy Hospital in the middle of the afternoon by C-section."*

This would have been my validation that the spirit was Jason. But . . . what if . . . the medium is just good at researching people before readings? What if they have a team of investigative reporters that work for free because, God knows, mediums should never charge for their services that are a *gift* from God? Hmmm . . . Still in my perfect world,

I would then want to hear from Jason: "I had squashed ears from being too cramped in there with Josh."

Okay, only our family knows this. So I've got my verification. But wait, to rule out the possibility that the medium is just picking up information telepathically from little ol' me, Jason would also have to add: "I hid my buck knife in a red metal box wrapped in a purple bandanna in the bottom left-hand drawer of the chest that was in my room, along with a signed note dated 7/22/1997 that is the date on which you will receive news of an upcoming wedding in the immediate family." I would then have to *find* that evidence and receive the news exactly as he said.

Okay, whew. Got it. Confirmation of this being my Jason talking to me. But . . . I still feel like something's missing. What could it be? I think I need to know that this is a link that will never break. That it will last as long as I am here and he is there. And I need to know that he really isn't *there,* but is *here.* So, I need to hear something like: "I'm doing fine, loving every minute of it, and will definitely be available to you whenever you so desire. I will not reincarnate and cease to exist all over again. I will not "move on" and leave you grieving again. I love you all very very very much and I am with you all the time, except when you're in the bathroom, naked, or having sex. Forever, eternally, always."

So now I'm happy. Perfect reading . . . perfect medium . . . perfect proof. I'm satisfied. No. I'm not. *It is a reality I don't want to face.* If I accept all of this as valid, it means that my son is no longer going to come through the door and ask what's to eat. It is the answer I wanted, but now that I have it, I want to continue searching for a *better* answer.

It is not a perfect world, at least it doesn't appear that way. It is a world created to give us the experiences we need to progress as loving and enlightened souls. The perfection comes when we remember why we're here and who we are.

The above narration is, of course, facetious. It is not the way mediumship works, at least not to my knowledge. If I would have had that kind of an experience when I first sat with a medium, I have no idea where my path would have led me next. It was the progression of readings, the different manners in which information was given and interpreted, the feelings that came with that first validation, the questioning, and the "ah-has!" that followed each reading that contributed to my healing and growth. Without that process taking place over the last three years, I believe I would be stuck back in a hole somewhere, high centered and spinning my wheels.

Before you contact a medium for a reading, there are a few guidelines I believe are important:

- ➤ Request references or testimonials. Any medium who is legitimate can come up with two or three satisfied clients who will share their experiences with you.

- ➤ Do get clear information on the cost of a reading and the usual amount of time involved.

> ➤ Ask about the medium's "philosophy."
> If they start spewing fear and evil, run,
> don't walk, the other way.

If all of the above feels good in your heart, it's time to schedule a reading. Before you go to the session, make the phone call, log into the chat room, or meditate. Spend a few minutes calming your emotions, clearing the stresses of the day, and asking your loved one to come through for you clearly.

Remember that whoever comes through is who needs to come through. If you have lost a child and you go in for a reading with your heart and soul depending on that child's appearance, you will be devastated when Uncle Joe and Great Aunt Sarah come bopping in to say "hi." Expect to hear validating information from *anyone* who is connected to you on the other side (or connected to you through the neighbor down the street who knows the man who passed in the car accident). Spirits will use whatever opening they can to get information through to those who need, and are ready to accept, communication from the other side.

Be open to whatever you receive, and remember that the information may not "click" until next week, next month, or even next year. But also be prudent and don't try to force something to fit when it wasn't meant to. Listen to your heart.

With all of the above, mediums also have what I call filters. Spirits present signs and symbols to get their message across. That message then has to be interpreted by the medium. An example: Jason once showed tropical foliage to a medium, after which she heard reggae music. She interpreted that as someone going to the islands. The next thing she heard was a word like *mercury,* and then *emery,* which made no sense at all to me. It all *clicked* a few days later when talking to my son Jeremy (*mercury . . . emery*), who worked in a juice bar called *Island Juice* where reggae music played all day and decorative palm trees graced the corners of the establishment.

Beliefs also come into play. If a medium believes that we reincarnate soon after we die, she may interpret a spirit not "showing up" as meaning that they have already returned to the Earth school. If a medium believes that each soul is met by an angel at the pearly gates, he may very well "see" that scene. I once had a medium tell me that souls who have passed through the light are unable to communicate with us. She told me that *if* (strong emphasis on that if) I truly felt Jason's presence, or heard from him through mediumship, I needed to know that he was still stuck (I can feel Jason laughing as I type this) on this side of the light. She believed this so strongly that she couldn't even consider that her thinking was wrong. Readings from this woman would most likely all involve assisting them toward the light since that is what she believed. Remember, we create what we focus on. Expectations and intent play a strong role in any spiritual endeavor.

I began exploring mediumship about three months into Jason's passing. I began talking to Jason (in my head) a few minutes after he passed. Sometime in the first couple of months, I began explaining to him that I needed to know he was okay. It became a nightly ritual to ask him for a sign or a message that would assure me of his continued existence and connection to us. I directed him to go to someone else if he couldn't get through my emotional garbage, and I suggested a few friends who might be open to that as well as a few reputable mediums I had read about. I was very specific and gave him names and locations. Having no idea how it all worked and no real conviction in Jason actually hearing me, I usually felt utterly insane the entire time I was talking to him. Insane, however, is preferable to hopeless. My dialogue with Jason was very specific and repetitive, always ending with, "Once you get their attention, just tell them to *call your mom!*"

Our first scheduled reading was with a medium from Canada. I found Donna on the Internet and e-mailed her before we decided to pay the nominal fee and set up an appointment for a reading. It was November, four months after Jason passed, and Dave and I set up speakerphones and a tape recorder to chronicle our first communication with Jason. I remember my voice shaking as I returned Donna's "Good evening," and recall being terrified that she would be unable to find my son. I had no proof of mediumship being valid, and worried that I was frantically grasping at straws.

After a chatty warm-up (undoubtedly designed to put us at ease . . . yeah, right), Donna "saw" a young man enter. The first thing he presented her with was a pair of huge hiking boots stomping around and around a miniature tree. If you have been reading every page, you will remember the ADC with the tree in our yard and the leaves that fluttered furiously with no perceptible wind.

Jason showed Donna that he was still "close to the Earth plane" and would not leave until he was "good and ready." He talked about our home that was also a school, and he stated he hadn't liked it there much. He showed hiking in the mountains with his dad, mentioned his brothers, and discussed how much fun he was having "making things happen." I believe it was Donna who heard Jason clearly say to me, "Stop looking up." There was more information, and the hour long reading was a good one to start with.

Jason hanging around and not going "to the light" seemed like something he would do. He assured Donna that this was a choice he was making and not a case of him being lost or "stuck" as some folks would like us to believe. Jason was stubborn in life, and there was no doubt in my mind that it was something he would be slow to lose. Dave and I work and live in a group home for adolescents. Jason was sick and tired of "bratty little high schoolers" for a few months before he died, hence the "not liking it there much." The "stop looking up" was most definitely a gibe because every time I talked to him I stared at the ceiling or the sky. I think he was telling me that wasn't necessary.

Although everything that Donna gave us was accurate and could fit Jason and our life with him, there was nothing that shouted out "This Is Me!" Donna knew the reading was lacking validity and e-mailed me a few days later. She shared that while sitting in circle, something mediums do as they are developing their skills, she had sensed a young male beside her. She had felt pain around her eyes. After the session, another medium who had sat across from Donna told her she had seen a young man standing to Donna's side. She said it looked like he had something wrong with his eyes. He had pretended to be playing the drums, and Donna speculated that perhaps it was Jason.

I believe it was. I think the eyes were his way of validating who he was since he had donated his corneas. As soon as I "got" this, I also "got" *my corneas, not my eyes*. I think the drum playing was due to his nickname of "Jazz." It felt right in my heart.

Our second reading (or attempt at one) was just before Christmas. A medium in California offered readings at no charge. What's to lose? Well, if I had been more vulnerable at that time and not cushioned by *The Fog*, it might have turned me completely around on the path. This is where I wish I had been given a set of dos and do nots when contacting a medium. I rang her up at the prearranged time and she attempted to find Jason on her "screen." She saw what appeared to be a background textured like strawberries. Yep, that's what she said. Strawberries. She then "thought" she saw Jason. She then started coughing and excused herself. About five minutes later, her roommate came on and told me that she was unable to go on with the reading and that she would e-mail me. She did. She "felt" that there was a block between Jason and us. She "felt" that one of us needed to forgive something before Jason would come through. This one "felt" like lead in my heart. I trashed it.

During the early months of 1997, I continued asking Jason daily to go to anyone who would listen and tell them, "Call my mom!" I had recently been introduced, via e-mail, to John Edward, a young and talented medium from Long Island. He had introduced me to Shelley Peck, another excellent medium, and I added both of their names to my nightly litany. "I *need* to hear from you, Jason. Go to John or Shelley. Tell them you're Jason and ask them to call me!"

During this same time period, I received two free e-mail readings with mediums I had met on a spiritual mailing list. Both of these women asked for Jason's first name, meditated, wrote down what they perceived, and then e-mailed it to me.

This is my reading from Lynn (my notes in bold):

"I saw him sitting on a wall I think and swinging his legs, impression of blond/fair hair, not very short although he says once it was VERY short. **(he shaved his head right before passing).** *Wearing smartish clothes, not sure what, obviously not that special. Told me of a time where he had to really be smart, a wedding or a big party?* **(both prom and a wedding in two months before**

passing). *Had a good time there, seems surprised he enjoyed it. Played some kind of sport or was keen on watching it, showing me a crowd cheering, also, funnily enough, ribbons of some kind, can't see the colour. Red flowers very clear. Seems to rush in and eat in snatches, enjoyed some food a lot but wouldn't touch others.* **(Both wedding and prom had red decor.)** *Showing me a big special meal—Christmas maybe? memorable for some reason . . . Showing me pizza with a load of topping* **(loved pizza)**, *says he liked the warm cozy times . . . Says he is now blowing your candles out and playing with your doors."* **(Remember the ADC in the last chapter?)**

Wendy sent this e-mail:

"I tried to contact Jason last night and this is what I got . . . He is being shielded . . . so perhaps the other psychic was correct to that extent. I saw him on a peaked roof . . . I got the impression that he got distracted, lost his footing and . . . that seems to be what he's apologizing for . . . not paying attention. He wants to be forgiven for leaving you so soon, but realizes that apparently it was his time to go. No one is ever ready to leave, and he (as you) were caught by surprise. He is "in school" now . . . learning and reviewing his life and what could have been done better. What you are "not supposed to know" is what his purpose was this time around . . . apparently it was fulfilled. He knows that now. He is happy and well, but very busy. And a bit surprised to be back in school. The message I received was that he loves you, and is sorry . . . please be gentle with yourself, and

go on with your life . . . he's busy but will be with you in spirit. . . . That was all I got . . . as I sit typing this now, I see him in jeans and he is waving . . . has a smile on his face . . . sort of crooked, as if he's happy, yet sad at the same time . . . it's a closed-mouth smile . . . did he do that often?"

Okay, Lynn's candle and door interpretation is significant because of the candle and door ADC I wrote about in the last chapter. In case you're confused about the sequence of events, the reading came first. Then the ADC. I am not convinced that Spirit can "predict" what will happen, but I do believe that time is very much a physical thing and has no meaning or logical place in the spirit world.

Wendy's message was good, but not very validating until she referred to his smile. The week before this reading, Dave and I had sat reminiscing while looking at pictures. Dave had gotten upset when he noticed that Jason didn't smile in any of his pictures when he knew it was happening. We surmised that it was because Jason needed braces and we had been unable to afford them before he passed. We bereaved parents can find all kinds of things to feel guilty about and this was a big one for Dave. It was the subject of a lengthy discussion between the two of us, and Wendy's mentioning his close-mouthed smile was a definite "bingo." I felt Jason smugly laughing at how clever he was in using that to validate the reading.

In February, I met a medium from Wales. Again, there was a nominal charge. We connected by

Internet and Laurence proceeded with a reading that was very good, very accurate, and very clear. He told us about a celebration at a lake with tents and campers and the names of Gary and Jerry. Jason had just missed (physically only) his annual ice-fishing derby that was always attended by his dad and two friends, Gary and Jerry. However, there were also several things that made no sense that left me feeling confused. I continued looking but kept this one, too. Each piece had a place to go in the puzzle.

I love this part. I am nearly as addicted to mediumship as my mom. But folks, you have to get a grip on what you're expecting. I can't believe some of the stories I've heard. Just the other day I watched a reading where a guy over here showed himself in a red football jersey to a great medium. I can hardly tell this story without laughing. The guy was a Nebraska fan; everything was red. Anyway, the medium said to his client, "He is wearing a red football jersey. Does that mean anything to you?" The client replied, "No. That can't be him; he was buried in a suit."

People, people, people! We have no bodies. We don't wear anything unless we want to, and even then it is seldom a suit. What we give for information to our mediums is given to validate who we are. It is a part of us. A memory, a name, a date, something we've recently shared with you, etc. We don't come through with code words that we agreed to give you when we passed, simply because those words were for our egos, which is the other thing we left behind when we died. You have to come to us, in your readings, or in your heart, with no expectations except to connect with love. Be open. Be willing to believe. Remember, as I said before, first you have to know it, then you can experience it. Believing is seeing.

13

Jason and John

Jason's Gift

When you left
You took the cool breeze of summer with you.
Rainbows paled, smiles became grimaces,
And the air I sucked into my aching soul was fetid and thick.
Prayers became jokes, faith turned to doubt,
And hope lay buried under a rock.
Sunsets came in browns and grays, muted by the dullness in
*   my soul.*
Then you returned. . .
Swooping into my heart, transforming my reality,
And bringing me truth—
*   A gift throbbing with the intensity of spirit.*
Now rainbows pulse with brilliance, breezes rustle emerald
*   leaves,*
*   And the air I breathe gently cools my burning soul.*
I understand that to know turquoise, I must first know grey.
And to know pink, I must understand brown.
I had to huddle in the black of an endless night
*   before I could grasp the radiance of a purple dawn*
Without sleep,
There is no awakening.
Without darkness,
. . . no light.
And without knowing the desperate, screaming agony of death,
*   I did not know life.*

— Sandy, July 6, 1997

IT WAS ALREADY HOT AND MUGGY ON JUNE 25, 1997. WE had been off for a few days and had just returned to work when the phone rang, and then the intercom. The call was for me, but our director had no idea who it was. I picked up the receiver.

"Hello, this is Sandy."

"Hi, blahndy, this is blah blah blah in blah eye land new blah."

"Excuse me? Who is this?" I asked. I was thinking I had a sales pitch coming up and I didn't have time to listen.

A bit clearer this time, and much slower, I heard "John Edward, in New York."

"Oh . . . Oh . . . Hi! Hello!" I (the blithering idiot) replied.

"Sandy, I was on a little R&R this past weekend and on Monday afternoon while lying on the beach, a young male came through and told me to *call his mom*. I believe that it was your son. Can I talk to you about that?"

"Oh, wow. Okay, yes, sure."

Oh My God!!! Yes!!! He Heard Me!!! Woooo-Hooooo!!!! Oh My God!!! Oh My Goddddddd!!!!

I quickly grabbed a pen and began scribbling notes as John proceeded with Jason's message.

John had felt the presence of a young male. He first heard "Call Mom" and then, "Sandy." He then heard "jsn," which he knows means Justin or Jason. Since this could have been a reference to a nephew named Jason, he left his lounge chair and called to check. All was well. He returned to his chair. Subtly, the young male appeared again. This time he said "orange slices" (John and I had discovered a mutual love of orange slice candies in a short chat a few weeks prior) and John made the connection. He asked Jason if the message had to come "*Now?*" and Jason said, "Yes." John asked, "Why me?" and Jason said, "Because Mom trusts you."

So John grabbed his pen and the hotel brochure, writing down all the symbols Jason showed him. A cap and gown **(Jason graduated two months prior to dying)**, Golden Books, a familiar shirt . . . all validating memories. John got a feeling of late teens **(Jason died at 18)** and saw a young male to Jason's side **(means friend or cousin)**, the letter "M," and cancer **(Jason's cousin Matt had died a few short months before Jason, and he had just received treatment for cancer)**. John also saw a grandpa, letter "R" **(Grandpa is Roy)** who liked to drink a bit **(yes)**. He talked about a recent occurrence with someone who looked like him **(his twin, Josh)**, clarified that his death was an accident, and said that he didn't get to talk to us before passing because we were "detained." **(Emergency room personnel would not let us in to talk to him.)**

He mentioned a wedding out of state and that the bride is pregnant **(Jason attended a wedding with us out of state a month before passing, and the bride was pregnant after this reading)** and also said "Happy Birthday" to someone in July **(Dave and Jeremy)**.

Jason was very insistent about the new dog, said that he is special **(new puppy, Otis)** and he drew John's attention to the cookies beside his chair—Otis Spunkmeyer Cookies.

John explained that Jason came through very strong, and very persistent. Like . . . "Do this for me, please!" He presented pink roses that means love, caring, and wellness. John said it felt like he "snuck in" but then came in loud and clear.

After John had given me the information Jason had shared at the beach, he asked me if we were at work. We were.

"Jason is with you. He is laughing that you don't have your coffee beside you **(I didn't)** and is showing me glasses. **(At that moment, my husband walked into the room and said, "Have you seen my glasses?")**. He is showing something to your left **(Jason's TV)** and that you are sitting at a desk. **(I was.)** *He is with you.* He is saying to look at my own birthday that is in October . . . who has a birthday in October?" **(me)**

"He says Happy Birthday to you. He seems extremely happy, Sandy, happy and relieved. He says he is not "there long" but is helping other young people cross over. He says you will be pulled into helping other moms. He mentions a "D" name. **(My publisher is Debbie.)** He says he is "one of three," which means he has two brothers **(yes)** and says 'hi' to his 'little' brother" **(his twin, a definite dig)**.

"He is with someone who has just drowned, a young male. He is saying he 'met' him and that he seized up in cramps or had a seizure." (**This was validated the week after . . . it was a friend of a friend, a young male in his 20s.**)

"He is saying this is your *proof.* Your spiritual vitamin. The path you are on is correct; you are doing the right things. He hears you and *he has not dropped the ball.* He says, 'Tell her I am all right. . . . I am fine.' . . . and he steps back."

With each word he shared, each validating point, every little nuance of Jason mentioned, I stepped up another rung on the ladder to the rooftop where I screamed out my news that Jason was still with us, still our son, and still very much a part of our lives. As I said later in a posting on the ADC message board, I had certainty!

I asked John to call us in a few days to attempt a reading that would be for Jason and his dad. I felt that Dave needed this and am sure that Jason was nudging me in that direction. John agreed, and two days later, on a Friday morning, John called us again.

First to come through was "your dad, Dave. I am getting an "R" (**Roy**). He is telling me that there is an anniversary or something in August or September and is showing me pink roses with thorns. This usually means there were problems, or issues to work through. He says you are five times the parent he was. He says to tell your brother 'hello,' and is showing me a beer mug" (**all accurate**).

"Someone with a "J" will have some health issues . . . (**my dad, J, had back surgery after this reading**), and there is another "R" here . . . your mother Sandy??? (**yes, Ruth**). Someone else with stomach problems (**my brother**), and they both say hi to 'J'" (**exact name. My dad's name is J.W.**).

"There is also a female cousin of Dave, I think. Catherine? Kathy? I think she is from mother's side Dave. Passed young, 30s or 40s?" (**Still unsure who this is.**)

"There are a *lot* of people . . . it's like taking attendance. Now they are parting energy and showing your son. He is telling me to tease Dave about something that happened that was embarrassing . . . showing himself very muscular again, manly sort of man."

"He says you are working in social work or health care? (**yes**) and wants to applaud your efforts. He says he never really paid attention before but what you are doing is great . . . *and* that there will be even more of this in the future. . . ."

"He says 'Hi' to someone who is missing a leg (**a friend, Gary**) and says he was to fly right after his passing (**yes**) and that Mom is going gambling. (**I was planning a women's trip to Reno at that time.**) He says, 'Dad's not going'" (**he wasn't, this was a ladies' trip**).

"It appears that Jason is involved as a liaison working with young people, a kind of educational experience, teaching. There is a young male by the name of Michael or Mark (**Matt?**) there with him. It is important to know that we can take a horrible experience and make something positive out of it. It is important for you, Dave, to hear that Jason is saying *he is okay.*"

"He is showing me your house, out back is something he wants to talk about **(after John had us draw our house and yard, we decided it was the garage).** He says he is there with you and thanks for the song." **(Dave works in the garage all of the time, always feels Jason, and always plays "Closer to the Light," a song by Bruce Cockburn.)**

"Someone has a purple heart? **(my brother, passed).** Now there is someone else, someone who shot himself, male, a connection to Ann or Anna, says to tell 'them' he is okay." **(I believe this is 'Chris' who you will meet later.)**

"Jason says again that he is one of three and 'hi' to his brothers. He says Mom was pregnant four times **(This is incredible . . . I had Jeremy [1], the twins [2], and a stillbirth that our boys were aware of [3]. However, I also had a miscarriage at six weeks that I know Jason was not informed of, at least not while he was in his *physical* life).** Did his brothers somehow mark themselves in his honor **(shaved heads before services)?** He mentions a family commitment by one of them soon, a marriage or birth. . . ." **(still waiting on this one but they are both engaged).**

"He says today is for you, Dad. He wants you to know he is fine, shows that he is bigger and taller than you . . . is laughing and teasing. He is proud of his body, his muscles . . . **(always)** and says that he is growing, evolving."

"He is saying that a family member was going to Denver with him but didn't go **(Josh and Jason** were supposed to go to Denver the day Jason died, to fly out and start boot camp and Josh didn't go, of course), and he is showing me again that he is with his grandpa, grandma, uncle, and someone in a coma . . . someone who died from impact to the body but had cancer" (cousin Matthew again).

"He is showing me Pepsi, Dave. Why is that? (Dave drinks at least a six-pack of Pepsi every day and often hid it from the boys). And with that, he steps back . . . he is gone."

Receiving all of this confirmation in one week was transcendent. The joy I felt was indescribable, and after telling my closest friends and family, I put the entire experience away for safekeeping. It was my joy, and I did not want to chance losing it.

Two months later, as the excitement of John's initial contact and follow-up communication began to fade, the sadness crept back in. I suppose it never really left, but was at least clouded for a while by the awe of Jason's contact. I realized that even though I now had confirmation of his presence in my life, it wasn't good enough. I needed to know that he would *always* be available to us and that he could hear me *whenever* I talked to him.

Sitting cross-legged at his Rock one afternoon, I had a long dialogue with him about my backslide into *The Pit*. I asked for another boost up the ladder to the rooftop, and after a few tears, I went home.

I checked into the chat room at **www.after-death.com**, didn't see anyone I knew, and left. After supper, I logged back on. Before I could even type "hello," the site's Webmaster informed me that John had been looking for me earlier. As I typed out the command to disconnect so that I could check my e-mail, John entered the channel. He had heard from Jason again and had a message to deliver. Although Jason had informed John he could find me in the chat room earlier, the log shows I had logged out five minutes before John logged on.

We moved into an empty channel so as not to be interrupted, and John began explaining Jason's fourth communication, which, interestingly, occurred on the 23rd of August just as the first contact took place on the 23rd of June. Once again, explanations are bolded and within parentheses:

The four of us **(John, Jason, Dave, and I)** began with "hello's" and "hey's" and John inquiring if I had read his e-mail. He was a bit startled at Jason's "coming through extremely polite and very subtle" after his rather brazen arrival at the beach. **(I smelled a little manipulation on Jason's part in that, but who am I to judge?)** I retrieved John's e-mail, scanned it, and immediately fell victim to psychic amnesia. If you have read Mr. Edward's book, *One Last Time*, you will remember that this affliction produces brief amnesia when we "mere mortals" are receiving messages from Spirit. However, after a bit of reflection, I recovered, and Jason's validations began falling into place.

After his gentle entrance into John's mind, Jason had shown John an October birthday. **(That would be mine.)** He had presented a paintbrush **(I had**

recently spent an afternoon painting our porch railing) and had given John the name of Chris or Christine. John felt that the unidentified Chris had passed recently. Jason spoke of an event coming up in October **(we were returning to our hometown)**, and then again referred to Chris, reporting his/her passing as "tragic and fast." He claimed to have greeted Chris on the other side, and though John could not determine Chris's gender, he did know he/she had passed at a young age. There was a New Jersey connection and a feeling that Chris was connected to someone I had been dialoguing with.

At that point in our chat, we all realized that Jason was "back" for another live reading. He remarked on Dave recently watching the movie *Ghost* and remembered that he had only watched parts, not all, of the movie **(all accurate).** Jason made reference to Dave drinking something red **(red beer in a red cup),** and then laughed hysterically about Dave "wearing or doing something feminine." **(Dave's legs were crossed at the knees, a pet peeve of Jason's.)** John then saw a shamrock, which typically symbolizes the month of March, and the 15th or 16th of that month. Jason told John again, doggedly, that he had Chris with him and that I would "connect with Mom soon." He then brandished a clear illustration of Snoopy, but this was no ordinary Snoopy asleep on top of his doghouse. This was a Snoopy . . . with erect ears. After suggesting it was a reference to our dog **(which is spotted like Snoopy)** and John's adamant "NO!," he asked,

"Is there a computer thing with a Snoopy near you?" There wasn't, at least not one that we could see, and Jason concluded by saying Chris had "died of an impact."

As Jason stepped back, I explained to John that I had sent out a plea for a spiritual boost just that afternoon. We discussed possible reasons for Jason contacting John, when it doesn't seem to happen so simply for others. John proposed that "maybe it happens for you so you can teach the others . . . share with them. . . ." He instructed me to "be sure and document all this for yourself. Time, date, messages, etc. Keep a log of all your experiences as well as these. I would have to think that they can benefit from your experiences." John then quoted Carol Burnett with her "I'm so glad we had this time together . . . ," reiterated that he "really did see Snoopy," and closed the chat room connection.

It is amazing that as many times as I have read the transcript for this reading, and after more than three years have passed, as I went through and put it into paragraph form, I found new validations in the messages John delivered. The reference that John made to documenting my experiences, along with thinking that the reason for my spontaneous contacts with Jason through John were going to be used to help others in similar situations, has to be about this book. When you read the epilogue, I think you'll agree.

John's reference to Carol Burnett could be just that. A reference. However, I find it interesting that

Jason has tugged on his earlobe in two readings I have had since. Carol acknowledged her family with an ear tug on each of her shows.

You read about a Chris or Christine. . . . Jason claimed he was with this person and had met him/her as they crossed over. John is unsure of Chris's gender and of the exact cause of passing. He is very clear that he/she was young, passed tragically, by an impact, and after Jason. He mentions March 15th or 16th, a connection to New Jersey, and a likely meeting with Chris's mom recently or soon. I believe that the Snoopy connection is also related to Chris.

Nearly three years after this reading, in June of 2000, I once again connected with Jason through John Edward. I will explain the particulars we received at that time regarding the mysterious Chris and *how* we obtained it. Trying to keep at least the highlights of this rambling book in chronological order forces me to leave it for you to ponder until you get to that point in the book.

In January of 1998, the After-Death Communication chat rooms hosted an exclusive chat with John Edward and Shelley Peck. The channel was packed, and every person invited had lost a child. John and Shelley shared the same computer for the online readings, and it appears that some of those who came through from the other side were sharing the same "microphone." It was a Wednesday night, and I remember that John had gone to pick Shelley up in one of New York's infamous snowstorms. We started late for those on the East Coast, but the time certainly didn't seem to affect the quality of John and Shelley's mediumship abilities.

Not too far into the chat, John stated that he was seeing *Calvin and Hobbes*. I immediately flashed on the unique stone at my nephew's grave and tried to remember the lines engraved under the *Calvin and Hobbes* characters. I typed in the window, "I have a nephew with Calvin and Hobbes on his headstone. . . ." *Headstone is such an ugly word.* John must not have seen what I typed, and he again repeated his earlier statement. Shelley then asked me if my nephew passed from a debilitating illness such as cancer to which I replied, "Had it, but didn't pass from it." Shelley felt that he would or could still be using it to identify who he was. I was excited to be making a connection so early in the evening. John then asked if anyone had received a bike in the last few months. *Oh, great, now he's asking me questions I can't validate and we're going to lose the connection. Damn. I'll just not answer. That's better than saying no.*

Shelley must have read my mind (imagine that, a psychic reading my mind . . .) because she typed, "He was younger than 14," and I had to say it wasn't him. *Sigh.* Before I could even take a break and shake my fingers out, John once again explained he was seeing Calvin and Hobbes and asked if anyone had lost a relative whose actions brought about their passing. The nephew I had been wondering about, Matthew, had passed in a car accident in which he was the driver and no other vehicles were involved. For whatever reason, at that point in the reading,

I didn't respond. It might have been that I didn't have time because when I next looked at the screen, John had stated, "I am also seeing two Jasons."

OMG! Okay, now we're cooking. . . .

John explained that the two came in together but were not related. He said that they are together on the other side and that one had Mary with him. By then, Susie, another mom from Wyoming, and I had both claimed "a Jason," and I jumped on the "Jimmy" or "Johnny" that was older, feeling pretty confident that Jason was acknowledging his older brother, Jeremy.

John heard 19, vehicle accident, close to a family birthday, and another holiday. Jason was nearly 19 when he died on the day after his dad's birthday and three weeks after the Fourth of July. Susie and I both remembered Marys on the other side about then, and it got rather confusing for us, and for John.

It appears now that a shift occurred and the "other Jason" began talking to John about his room and other items that would validate his presence for his mom. I sat back and listened, thinking my Jason was already gone. After that was accomplished, John heard an "R" name, someone in the family. Susie and I both had "R's" on the other side, and then John heard "Roy," and I was back in the ball game. John commented that both boys were talking at the same time and asked if one of them had a uniform connection. Jason would have been in the Navy the day he died, and the "Roy" we had identified had been in the Marines.

John went on with, "Okay—one of the Jasons is talking about his heart . . . not being able to handle his situation . . . but I don't think this is a medical problem. . . ." Jason died because of the damage that the electricity did to his heart. We then went back to, "Is one of the Jasons connected to the Calvin and Hobbes thing? I am being shown that again." *Oh, my. I don't think he heard me. Uh-Oh.*

Now, if this had happened in the Gallery on John's *Crossing Over* show, I think I might have been asked to leave. Those of you who know (and love) John, know that he has the utmost respect for spirit. He wants them to get their message across. Unfortunately, it takes not only them sending the information, but also us receiving it. It was obvious to me that John had not seen what I had typed earlier about Calvin and Hobbes. It should have been obvious to me to clarify that by saying, *"I told you that . . . etc."* But oh no, not me. I simply typed, "No . . . only that Jason's cousin died and has it on his head-stone . . . same grandpa."

If you can hear a pin drop in a chat room, I heard it.

"Wait . . . so your Jason has a cousin with the Calvin thing on his headstone . . . and you don't find that significant?" *Uh-Oh.*

John then explained to the entire room about spirit getting our attention and how they do that. I tried to explain that he hadn't seen what I'd typed earlier, but it wasn't changing the fact that I hadn't been clear and insistent in my answers.

Jason let John know that he is with "this other Jason. . . ." and that it was important we know they are together. He told John they had more in common than their names, and one of them mentioned a grandmother passing from a heart condition. Since both of our mothers fit that information, John asked Susie if she had her mother's rings or something sentimental near her. She did, and Susie's Jason was back at the mic.

After several validating messages from the other Jason, John asked, "What is wrong with his hair?" in reference to Jason's dad. He felt it was funny and was to acknowledge it. Susie couldn't understand the reference and I did. They've passed the mic again. "Did his Dad do something with him after he passed regarding his hair . . . or something he points to the head." Dave had just received a horrible haircut. Funny-looking was a wonderful description. There was another reference to a Mike, "Who is Michael? He calls out Mike. We may be off . . . by the sound . . . not the initial . . . he is talking about a male M. Feels like a male figure to the side . . . bro/friend . . . etc. And he talks about Dad's hair . . . did he just get it cut? or something? He knows what he is trying to say." I know this was Jason introducing the owner of the *Calvin and Hobbes* stone. Too bad he didn't do it earlier in the night. The readings went on for others, but ours was finished, and once again, I was thrilled.

As I read through the chat log while writing this chapter, I found things that should have made sense to me then and didn't. Having heard from Jason several times by then, I think I must have felt gluttonous. When I wasn't certain about a message, I often stayed quiet for fear of staking claim to someone else's loved one.

Reflecting back on the events from November of '96 through January of '98, I can see that Jason was as intent upon giving as I was upon getting. I believe that my focused and almost ritualistic request of him to find a way through only strengthened the bond between us. I think of it as a chord of energy, with each thought I sent adding strength and intensity. As I added John Edward to the list of those I trusted as messengers, a circle of energy connected by that chord of light was formed.

First of all, since Mom forgot to tell you, John has written three books that should be on everyone's bookshelf. You'll find them listed in the back of this book. I "met" Mr. Edward when he was just a pup, but his message to communicate, appreciate, and validate has since opened up doors for all of us. His integrity and respect for spirit is amazing. Thank you, John. From all of us.

Okay, this period of time (yours of course, not mine) was so awesome. Mom had been so committed to talking to me nightly and I wanted nothing more then to follow through with what she was asking of me. Finding John Edward open and willing to listen was incredible. After four times in less than a year, though, I figured it was time to move on. John was needed elsewhere, and I had plans for Mom. I put the Chris person on hold, and decided it was time to answer the woman who had cried out to the universe on the same night my mom did. Both were asking for signs; both were wanting to know so much more than they did. . . . I had remembered who this lady was, and I found her doing a reading online while my mom watched, so I did what I do best. I opened up the space between them and let the energy flow. It was time for them to meet and begin a new chapter in their lives. I could hardly wait to get started, and as it turned out, I didn't have to.

14
Jason and Ocallah

Illusion

Sitting here under the stars,
wrapped in your afghan,
I search for signs of you.
A shooting star,
a breeze in the stillness,
a light drifting toward me.
As tears blind me,
I turn off the pain by going elsewhere,
somewhere before now.
When I return
there is a fleeting moment
when I look down the street
in the direction you last walked,
and instead of agony
I feel anticipation
as I wonder what time you'll return
and what you'll want to eat.

— Sandy, 1996

EVEN WITH JOHN AND SHELLEY'S INCREDIBLE READING, that second winter without Jason seemed to last forever. Whereas we had confirmation of Jason's continued existence, it was a reality we were reluctant to accept. I continued looking for fellow travelers on the unending road before me.

One of the largest metaphysical sites on the Web, Spirit Web, drew my attention. I visited once or twice a week, and on about the fourth visit, I was fortunate (or guided) to witness a medium giving her first online reading. "Ocallah" was obviously gifted, and after seeing her tell a young woman that her brother (in spirit) was reaching toward her light switch, at which time the sister's lights flickered, I was hooked. I asked for a reading, and we made arrangements to meet later in the week. The free reading went off as planned, and Jason came through loud and clear with validating (and a few confusing) messages. Ocallah and I became chat buddies. We met often to discuss both spiritual and physical events. After a couple of weeks of chatting, I talked her into visiting the chat rooms I usually went to, and we moved from Spiritweb to the After-Death Communication server. Ocallah was soon offering free readings to those in need.

One evening in February, a fellow chatter asked where everyone was located. There were 20-some folks assembled, and New York, Philadelphia, and Missouri appeared on the screen. As I typed Wyoming out on the keyboard, I was amazed to see it pop up before I hit the enter key. Since we are known for having more antelope then people, the odds of two people in an after-death chat room being from Wyoming are astronomical. Just as I was typing "Where in Wyoming?," Ocallah private-messaged me.

Ocallah: "*You* are from *Wyoming?*"

Sandy: "Yeah, why?"

Ocallah: "*So am I!*"

Sandy: *"Whoa!* Where?"

Ocallah: "Jackson. Where are you?"

Sandy: "Do you know where Red Top Meadows is?" **(Red Top Meadows is the name of a facility for at-risk youth in northern Wyoming. The area it is in is also Red Top Meadows.)**

Ocallah: "Oh my God! I live in Red Top Meadows!"

Sandy: :) **(that's a smile)**

The story goes on, but essentially it was one of those coincidences that can't possibly be a coincidence. We became friends, and Jason had a voice.

The year progressed, as did I. I introduced Ocallah, who's real-world name is Cyntha Craton, to my friends on the Internet, and she introduced me to her friends in spirit. She amazed me. It was during this first year of knowing Cyntha that my need to pursue contact with Jason lessened in intensity. It became apparent that Jason would show up when he had something to share. I should have figured this out when he went to John, but I was still very needy at that time, and I think Jason understood that.

In the beginning, I looked for someone who could ascertain Jason's existence. I wanted to hear what he was doing, how long he would be doing it, was he okay, was he still my baby. Drowning in hopelessness and focused on my own needs, I had little interest in what others received. I wanted to hear from Jason. Now, four years into this journey, my attraction to mediumship has changed. It is now the joy on a mother's face and the tremor in a Dad's voice that pulls me in. I now understand that a message for one is a message for all.

Cyntha and I chatted nightly. We could be discussing the weather or a show on television, and in would pop Jason. Sometimes he brought serious philosophical information, sometimes rocketing validations, and sometimes utter nonsense. Both he and Cyntha grew in their abilities to communicate through the veil between our world and theirs.

During one of our chats, Cyntha mentioned a vivid memory of another night much like the cool, breezy one we were experiencing. She recalled sitting on her porch during the fall of 1996, gazing through tears toward the sky, and asking for answers. She felt lost and unsure of what she was here for and wanted a sign that would say to her—*There is more than this.* She remembered pleading for assurance that life had meaning beyond what she could see.

Click. I remembered a night during the same fall, a night much like the one Cyntha described. I recalled sitting under the stars wrapped in Jason's afghan. Curled in the fetal position, I begged to know more than this. I pleaded for assurance that life had meaning and that death was not an end. Was it possible that Jason had "heard" both of us? Could he have something to do with our chance meeting?

I am going to include bits and pieces of the messages that Jason funneled through Cyntha. These contacts began in January of 1998 and continue today. I will put them in chronological order so that you can see how Jason changed in regards to the information he was giving and how he gave it.

I have already referred to this first one, but I think it's significant that you see how names and words come through for different mediums. You will remember John saying that "it might be off in the way it sounds, but it won't be off by initial." Cyntha, on the other hand, began getting names and words strictly based on the "way it sounds." Here's a snippet of an early reading.

Cyntha typed, "He says, 'You tell her I've got six digits . . . mercury. . . .' something about a volcano . . . are you planning Hawaii or something like that? I'm seeing a lot of tropical imagery . . . talking about a guy . . . emery . . . he's loading me with sounds and names."

As soon as I heard Emery, I also heard Jeremy. I didn't relate to the imagery she was seeing, but I knew it had something to do with Jeremy and later validated the message when Jeremy explained his workplace decor.

Cyntha went on with, ". . . am hearing reggae music, he drags a rake over Jeremy's head, did Jeremy do something to his hair? Is Jeremy in army/navy? Way short . . . says 'tell him I was here. . . .' and says a pet name like 'big baboon' . . . and laughs so hard, bending over laughing, says I got it right. 'Mom's like an addict, goes through withdrawal without me, with love, Mom's so sad.' . . . he says he has to make you laugh. 'I love you, Mom' . . . waves good-bye with his fingers . . . like drumming them in the air. That's it."

Jeremy had his head shaved for Jason's funeral. The "big baboon" is simply Jason teasing his older, but smaller, brother. Note how the information is strictly to validate (or strictly silly) with no strong spiritual content.

Okay, here's the next one I want to share. This was toward the end of 1998 and went from silly to emotional. I felt it coming, and when the kite reference came up, I nearly vibrated with the energy Jason was putting out. I suspect that the energy was in the love between us and not in the words Cyntha was typing, so you may not be able to feel what I was feeling. You'll have to take my word for it.

Cyntha first heard *tickets*. I had no idea what that meant and told her so. Jason once again showed her, "... tickets ... you have some tickets ... tickets, tickets, tickets ... rayovac, rayovac. Says he always plays games ... crayon ... are you drawing a sign? I see crayons. ..."

So far, Jason was batting a zero.

Cyntha went on with "... said you are cooking his food, tomorrow ... are you? Says 'yum' ... let me see if I can see what it is ... I see a casserole dish and what looks like elbow noodles in it. I hear 'manicotti' but I see elbow. ..."

I verified that Jason's favorite lunchtime meal was macaroni and cheese. Still being silly, he went on with, "Thanks, Mom, I'll be there, too."

Cyntha observed him grabbing the salt shaker, "... it needs salt ... he says a prayer ... with his silverware in his hand ... banging on the table ... 'good grub ... let's eat!'"

That would be Jason. Our boys were not very religious. ...

Cyntha continued, "His shoelaces are untied, tennis shoes, Velcro too, zzzzzzzip, could this be a memory of some kind? Bangs his head on table when he comes up from under it, food fight, fling, Jeremy. . . ."

All of these are memories, childhood scenes of growing up with three brothers. Now, as you read the next section, try to feel the energy shift.

". . . kite . . . flying a kite . . . *kite in wires* . . . someone cuts the rope . . . Jason takes it . . . runs with it . . . so happy . . . running . . . running . . . smiling . . . looking up at the kite . . . Otis barks at him . . . chases him . . . barking . . . looking up, too . . . look up Sandy . . . tomorrow . . . the sun will come out . . . look up . . . he shows you letting balloons go in the air . . . says 'thank you, got it' . . . blows out candles . . . puts frosting on his nose . . . smiles at you all . . . 'I love you Mom' . . ."

After this reading, I realized that less than an hour before, I had been using markers to write on a wipe-off board on our bed in our bedroom. Right beside the wipe-off board, on the same bed, were Jeremy's airline tickets to fly home for Christmas. Right beside those tickets was a brand new package of Rayovac batteries.

It "felt" like the kite represented Jason and his injury. The cutting of the ropes, to free the kite (i.e., Jason) was me at the hospital saying please let him live, don't let him die, and then toward the end, saying whatever is best for him, he is what matters. . . . He was then "free," no restrictions, flying high.

I have no idea why Otis was there. Perhaps to say that Otis could see him or to link the past with the present? The balloons had been released that same day for his birthday, and the cake and frosting was of course in reference to that same event.

I was feeling the Christmas spirit a little in 1998, our third one with Jason in spirit, and was excited about the National Children's Memorial Day and the candle lighting that would encircle the globe. Cyntha had agreed to host a special chat for the occasion, and nearly a hundred people gathered in the chat room for messages from their children. I was helping moderate the room and didn't really expect Jason to show up. I knew there were others more needy than I. However, I let him know that a visit would be very okay by me and that he would have to be pushy to get Cyntha to acknowledge him. It seems that every time a medium becomes a friend, of mine and of Jason's, they become wary of doing readings for us. They begin feeling as if they know too much to give validating information. What they don't understand is that I am past the stage of needing confirmation. I know Jason. When he comes in, it doesn't matter if he is green and purple with a Southern accent. I can feel my son's presence.

As we gathered in the chat room, I had a private window open with Cyntha, and soon after the opening prayer, another private window was open to another friend, Nixie. I would like to give you the exact details of how the entire evening went, but I would have to combine the three transcripts into one. That being nearly impossible, a short narration will have to suffice. The synchronicity of the entire event was amazing.

Before the chat began, I invited Jason to the festivities. I envisioned him dressed in black pants, white shirt, holding a little dark-haired boy's hand, and standing in front of a crowd of thousands of children and young adults. They were in an outside setting and each held a candle high in the air, some already lit, some not.

When Nixie came in and privated me, she announced that Jason, dressed in black and white, had "swooped in and led me to my computer." She saw a little boy with him and what resembled "an outdoor concert with everyone holding their Bics in the air."

Meanwhile, in the main window, Cyntha came through with a message from Jason and talked about him having a young dark-haired boy with him. She saw Jason dressed in black and white. Later on, I "heard" Jason say a little girl wanted to be next. Within a few minutes, Nixie, Cyntha, and another medium in the chat all felt a little girl trying to make a connection.

I have never felt such magic in the air as I did that night when children from all over the world held their candles in the air and connected with their parents.

Before reading the next paragraph, I need to clarify that Cyntha did not "hear" Jason say all of this. This is the first of several readings that were delivered via what I would call automatic writing. It seemed to Cyntha that she just allowed Jason an opening and he "typed" the words for her. It is also the first of several messages that appeared to be for anyone needing to hear it.

Cyntha told me she had Jason and that he felt different. She could only describe it as, "He does seem to have a new feel, like . . . higher." She said he was pacing back and forth and showing her "cliché imagery" of heaven. She saw a gate, clouds, and walking on clouds. She heard him say, ". . . heaven. most people dream of it like this, like people looking just the same, only whiter, cleaner. . . ." He then showed that they do not look like that. In a flash he showed himself turning into a small point of light and then back again to his original image. He pointed to the sun, then to himself as a tiny beam of light, mentioned rays and something about how the sun projects everywhere.

As I was reading through the message Cyntha was typing, I was thinking, *Who is this? This could be anyone. Anyone but Jason who talks about Rayovac and tickets.*

"Stop . . . Mom . . . stop thinking. . . ."

Uh-oh. Here we go. . . . Okay, then how do I know this is you?

"By not thinking. Just feel."

Sigh. . . .

Now that he had gotten my attention, Jason showed Cyntha a hand held palm facing up and sunlight on the palm. She then saw an image of me, looking at the light on my hand and up at the sun. As she tried to type what she was seeing exactly as she was seeing it, I was getting those zzzziiinnnnggggsss that say *pay attention*. Jason was taking over Cyntha's computer.

"Which is which? You can't think it, you can only feel it. Warm, hot, sun, here, there, and in between. I'm there . . . and here . . . and in between . . . which reminds you of me? The sun, the ray, the warmth, the heat on your face? Which one am I? At first I thought I was a tiny star, all alone, then I saw I am a part of the bigger star, and then I knew I was also the ray, and just because a cloud comes along, doesn't mean I am gone. I'm hidden from view, but I am the same. The light . . . even light reflecting from the moon, see? No . . . don't think, feel it. Warms you inside, just remembering. Mom sweats, heat builds, and radiates to her body. She says, I feel hot . . . energy in motion, constant."

"When you chill, I am there. It's because I slow down so much. Coolness . . . slowed energy. Heat . . . raised energy. Don't think about it . . . when you go to sleep your body cools because the source of energy has retreated . . . sort of."

"Energy touches . . . sense me in the air but when I come to you I come from within you . . . within that place. That is where I am . . . in that part of you that is also that part of me. In your soul, spirit, memory. Doesn't matter what you call it, God . . . mind . . . heart. See . . . it starts from that place."

"When you feel my arm, the feeling is my memory. I connect to yours and then, only then, you feel it, in your body . . . because I put the thought there in the first place, but it took you to notice it, physically . . . to say *Jason*."

"Mom, I love you. Feel this, feel my memory across your skin . . . kiss, shhhhhh, Dad's experience of me was real. Your experience of me is real, so which is the sun? Which is the dream? Is this heaven? Or is the memory heaven? Or is it all inside you still, because you never forgot the truth? godisloveandsoareyou . . . iwanttogohome . . . you already are. Night Mom. Night Dad. Next time . . . youwillknow."

What can I say about this message . . . that it was incredibly validating? No. That it was proof of my son's spiritual development? No. I can only tell you what I felt. As the words tumbled out onto my screen at breakneck speed, I felt love. Pure, unconditional love. Here was the "child" I had raised, the boy I had taught numerous life lessons to, teaching me about life. And not once did he tell me to get a clue.

A few weeks later Jason popped back in for a chat with Cyntha and me. He began by showing Cyntha, ". . . him and Josh going off on their own, through the woods . . . running . . . laughing . . . like they are playing a game . . . hiding from you . . . I hear 'my side of the mountain' . . ."

Okay, cool, that's pretty significant. Jason had made his Dad and I smile when (at 16) he informed us that he planned "to run away" when he turned 18. He wanted to live off the land on his own mountain.

We had teased him about it until it became a family joke.

Cyntha went on with what she was perceiving. "I see the character living in his own hut, eating from the land, water, acorns . . . a deer comes . . . walks right up to Jason . . . Jason's hand is extended to the deer . . . the deer licks his hand . . . Jason strokes its neck . . . I hear forgiveness . . . I want to cry for some reason."

Before Cyntha had typed "I want to cry for some reason." I had felt the familiar lump in my throat and both my eyes were full of tears. She went on with what she called "a huge download."

". . . now Jason looks into the water . . . and sees himself . . . reflecting . . . okay . . . the story of Narcissus . . . the Greek legend . . . mother in the mirror . . . in the mirror . . . wipe the steam . . . does 'Berry' mean anything?"

Whoa, this is definitely significant. Jason does this often. I think he feels my denial kicking in, the little voice that says, "A kid who used self-tanner as hand lotion cannot possibly turn philosophical this fast!" So he throws me something black and white that shouts, "Yes, indeedy! It is I!" Berry was a classmate of Jason and Josh's throughout their entire time in Wyoming. She had been murdered in the fall of 1996 and her mother and I are Compassionate Friends. I had asked Jason more than once if he had "seen" Berry. Okay, back to the reading.

". . . he's on the roof . . . that roof . . . that night . . . looking up . . . with his friends . . . he stands up

. . . there is a bright star . . . he points to it . . . 'I'm going there' . . . like that . . . now the Lion King and Mufasa in the sky . . . and the entire message . . . of the circle of life . . . and the mountain . . . 'I once had a dream I would be a great person. . . . I am still a great person . . . even now' . . . 'Sound of Music' . . . the song . . . 'Climb Every Mountain' . . . ."

Jason continues "typing" for Cyntha. "You see . . . I had a nightmare as a child . . . you remember? A huge fear . . . of death . . . of leaving you . . . of leaving. You came to me . . . you told me . . . 'I am here . . . it's okay. . . .' Mom, I am here . . . it's okay. . . . Mom . . . this nightmare is over now . . . waken . . . I am here . . . it's okay. . . ."

Once again, the feeling was overwhelming. The tears leaving rivulets on my face were not from sadness, but from the joy of knowing my son was present. As I blew my nose, I asked him—*but will you always be here, Jason? Forever?*

And Cyntha typed, "He says yes! I love you, Mom . . . Dad. . . ."

Thank you, Jason, thank you . . . thank you . . . thank you!

And Cyntha typed, "You're welcome, Mom."

Will you have to leave again ever?

And Cyntha typed, "No . . . I'm not going to leave you. . . ."

She continued. "I see an image of the ocean . . . the water . . . the tide . . . in . . . out . . . rolling on the shore . . . only appears to leave . . . but is never far . . . like the waves. . . . Dad knows . . . he heard from me today . . . you ask . . . he felt me . . . there . . . I heard him . . . talk to me . . . goodnight, Mom. . . ."

The next message came about after I told Jason thank you and "You've given me a million gifts by dying." This was the first of many times when Cyntha and Jason appeared to carry on a two-way dialogue and the second time that Jason appeared to be talking through Cyntha's daughter, Annie. (Note that Jason says at the very beginning, "Give me a voice." and then seems to talk through Annie.) You'll also notice Jason always gets in the last word.

Cyntha had already alerted me to Jason's presence, and began by typing, ". . . he said 'make my presents known.' Not presence, but presents!?"

"Wow." I typed. "Presents = Gifts. Interesting. When I was at his rock today, I was talking to him, and I said, 'Thank you . . . you have given me a million gifts by dying.'"

Cyntha went on delivering what appeared to be a "Lesson from Jason" on life after death. I will use italics to depict what Cyntha is "thinking" to Jason.

". . . give me a voice . . . people want to know the answer to 'How do you know?'"

Cyntha answered Jason with—*I know because it's been my experience.*

"And this is mine. I wouldn't have known how to reach you if it hadn't been for Mom calling me. She gave me a voice by calling out to me, telling me it's possible. Reach me."

How do we know we're not just making you up?

"How do you know you're not just making your Self up?"

I don't.

"Yes, you do."

I do?

"Yep. . . ."

Hmmm. Well . . . I guess I know I'm not making myself up because I am conscious.

"How do you know that?"

Cuz I can touch and see and feel and hear, cuz of my senses of who I am.

"I'm no different. I touch, see, feel, hear. . . . I hear you. I touch Mom."

So what would this book be about? And do you even care if we write it?

Cyntha and I were toying with the idea of co-authoring a book. I'm not so sure we're not still toying with the idea.

"Let it be about your experience of me and of spirit and of love and life and don't forget to laugh."

But death is serious to people.

"So is life, but you laugh about that. Listen to your daughter. . . ."

Cyntha explained to me that Annie was in the bathroom and was talking to herself. She started typing exactly what she heard Annie saying.

"I just don't know if I'm ready to see yet. I just don't know. But . . . but no one knows . . . only me and, oh my God! God I'm so alive! I see him. I wish they would come . . . oh my God . . . we won't even think about it . . . it's too weird . . . just think . . . mean . . . I won't leave you anymore."

Soon it was late in the summer of 1999, and Jason had this to share.

". . . shows me Easter, eggs, trees, yard, dirt road, group home, jelly beans, licorice . . . points to licorice. He says 'yum.' He says oyster, pearl . . . white jelly bean in his pocket. . . ."

"You find these only after an irritation forms around a painful thing . . . beautiful, sweet . . . if you could dissolve the sweetness . . . layer by layer, back to the moment of pain . . . the irritant, you would not have the preciousness, to adorn you, like a pearl."

Cyntha and I spent some time pondering what a jelly bean has in common with a pearl, but Jason wouldn't wait for us to finish. Jason showed her a wave rolling into the shore, and an oyster on the sand, and my coming along and finding it. He explained:

". . . it is so ugly, so covered in algae and grit, but you take the time to open it, to explore it, and discover something so beautiful within, you are that. . . ."

"Mom, look what you've found, so beautiful within that pain, from that, radiant, you . . . that's my mom . . . I chose her for this . . . this walk on the shoreline, sweetness. . . ."

He showed Cyntha an M&M again, a white jelly bean, a licorice one, and a pearl . . . and Cyntha and I were both entirely lost. We simply did not see a connection between jelly beans and pearls.

But Jason continued—"But you will, because you know . . . how to look . . . with your heart . . . I love you, Mom."

I typed "I love you, Jason" in the window (which is really stupid because it's not like he's sitting somewhere on a computer reading what I type), and Cyntha asked me if I knew a Danny. She had heard what sounded like, "Tell Danny I said hello."

Not knowing a Danny, I was pretty sure Jason was saying "Daddy," and sure enough, the next message validated that clearly.

". . . coonskin cap, singing, Davy . . . Davy Crockett . . . he shows wearing one as a boy . . . giggling in the backseat of a car . . . throwing jelly beans at the back of Dad's head . . . ping . . . giggle . . . ping . . . snicker. . . ."

Not until now, as I am writing this paragraph, do I "get" the connection between pearl, oyster, and jelly bean. Jason was occasionally an irritant. The jelly beans were irritants on the car trip. But it is the irritants that create layers and layers of memories, which create pure beauty. *I've got it. Yes!*

Cyntha hears . . . "Are we there yet?"

She sees a road trip . . . a station wagon.

Once again Jason comes through with a black and white validation in the middle of a spiritual discourse. Station wagon . . . go figure. I'm surprised Jason chose to "go public" with this information.

Jason shows having to ". . . stop . . . again . . . has to pee . . . sorry . . . he made me say it! He's silly."

He then says, "Remember? What irritated you then is so beautiful now, in memory . . . irritants . . . beautiful . . . sweet . . . don't take it back. When you would be frustrated and irritated with me, they are precious memories, I love them, too. I liked to get Dad frustrated like that, because, then Dad "saw" me, had to stop, pull over, turn around, face me, talk to me, connect with me, one-on-one, face-to-face . . . Dad loved me . . . loves me . . . love sometimes is like that, don't take it back, or wish it away, or regret any of it."

He showed Cyntha the bite mark on his brother, said it is his permanent smile, and pointed to my heart, saying, "There is yours . . . I'm all grown up now, but still your boy . . . sweet boy . . . sometimes irritating . . . frustrating . . . painfully so. . . ." Jason saluted Dave and stepped back. . . .

Late one night in September of last year, I asked Jason to tell me about the night he died. I told him I realized he might not even remember it, but that if he did, I'd like to hear his perception of the entire event. I explained my need to know what he was aware of and who he had been met by on the other side.

I logged into the chat room later that night and found Cyntha waiting for me. She knew we were going to try contacting Jason and that I had a question already on the way to him. She had no idea, however, what that question was or even what it was related to. She asked me to focus on the question and on Jason, and once again I repeated in my head— *Tell me about the night you died. If you can remember* . . . Cyntha began typing.

"He is saying how, if they want to, they can recreate anything, any experience on Earth. I don't know if that has meaning, but I'll just let it flow. He says they also can relive any experience in order to learn from it. Like, if you didn't get it the first time and you are in spirit, you can recreate it from the new perspective you now have. If they want, things they didn't understand about an experience in life they can relive to see it correctly."

Wow. I think he heard me. That was certainly an answer to the not remembering part. Wow.

". . . shows me the wire . . . shows me how he could relive that, see it clearer, to understand . . . he helps people in spirit to do just that and he says he can go to the places he never got to go to in life . . . I am suddenly seeing his life flash before my eyes, like quick pictures, like one image per half second . . . my middle back is aching, on the left side, and my left leg . . . I now feel dizzy . . . are you asking him about what he felt when he passed?"

I answered Cyntha in the affirmative and watched as more words came up on my screen.

"I'm going very fast . . . lots of colors . . . I have no control over it . . . the feeling of speed . . . I keep seeing this indigo color . . . like a rich . . . rich blue . . . royal blue sort of . . . but darker . . . I see what looks like lightening flickers . . . in this energy tube . . . sparks . . . I hear his emotions . . . woah! woah! woah! . . . and totally unable to stop."

This is too incredible.

"Okay, he shows this. He shows it suddenly, immediately stop. He is in a field, and then shows me Wizard of Oz . . . how Dorothy opened the door to color and it is so quiet and so peaceful and so breathtaking. He looks behind himself, like he's looking for someone or something, and Gary is there.

Cool . . . Gary. Cyntha had already met my brother Gary in a reading before this one.

Cyntha then felt a conversation between Jason and his Uncle Gary that went something like this:

"Look . . . they're going to freak out about this."

"Then do something good with it."

"You've got to be kidding, I'm not done."

"Nope. That's true. You've only just begun."

Cyntha types more. "Flashing again, lots of energy, moving . . . moving fast. Did you get a phone call? When he passed . . . did you pick up the phone?"

I had.

"That's what he showed me . . . moving fast again . . . moving . . . moving . . . click . . . click . . . images . . . time . . . energy . . . in hospital . . . looking at himself . . . 'breathe breathe!!!' . . . he hears murmured voices in the room . . . he hears what sounds like 'ice pack!' . . . he sees them packing things around his body . . . around his sides . . . feet are freezing cold . . . legs cold . . . blood feels like mud . . . so thick . . . 'breathe, breathe, breathe!!!' . . . click . . . click . . . flashing energy again . . . looks like ice packs . . . and dark 'blanket' type thing . . . maybe . . . was a tourniquet on his legs . . . my lower legs are totally numb/cold feeling. . . ."

All of the physical symptoms Cyntha has mentioned fit Jason's injury. His cause of death was extangiation or internal bleeding.

". . . was on respirator . . . bag . . . was doctor a middle-aged man . . . partly bald or thin hair on top . . . shows him in hallway . . . hears 'I'm sorry, we're doing everything we can . . . chances are . . . organs damaged . . . suffering long-term effects' . . ."

"Flashing again, moving again . . . Josh in view . . . Dave in view . . . emotions pouring from Jason . . . 'I'm sorry . . . I'm sorry . . . shit . . . I can't handle this!' . . ."

"Looking for Gary . . . looking behind himself again . . . it stops . . . it soothes . . . back in that field . . . small stream . . . sitting on a log . . . hands over face . . . Gary's arm around his shoulder . . . very comforting. I hear the water . . . then I realize I see the water . . . I can touch it . . . put hand in it . . . and it feels almost hot . . . startling sensation . . . like feeling the very life force of the water. . . . Gary tells him 'Everything there, is also here in its (etheric) form.' I couldn't understand the word he just used but I felt the meaning . . . now I see balloons . . . were there balloons at his funeral . . . kids . . . cars . . . trucks . . . streamers . . . things hanging off a truck . . . in back. . . ."

There were balloons, lots of balloons, but no streamers that I am aware of. I think this was just Jason's way of showing his passing as a time to celebrate.

". . . some of them understood even before I did that it was a celebration, something to be happy about . . . I couldn't, though . . . I asked Gary, 'How can you be so *happy*, man! You're *dead*!'"

"Gary said, 'You'll see, my man.'"

"That's where my (enthusiasm) kicked in. I pushed you Mom, pushed you to this . . . to finding this . . . you thought you pushed me . . . (to John Edward) . . . but it was *me* . . . and now we are in this together . . . she's (meaning Cyntha) just willing

and a nut . . . like me. I fit 'in' well with her energy
. . . and, because you doubt so much when I am with
you, I chose her . . . she called . . . I came. . . ."

"Okay, he stopped."

Thank you, Jason.

The change of seasons always triggers memories
I had left stored away the year before. After a hard day
in May, I told Jason I was sorry for being such a
sniveling whiner. I had let fear rear its ugly head
again and was feeling Jason moving away (or staying
away) due to my emotional negativity. That evening,
he tapped Cyntha on the shoulder and delivered
the following:

"'There is no 'where I am not', nothing that keeps
me from you . . . I am not too busy, too taken with my
new life . . . and there is nothing you could ever do
that would keep me from making my presence known
to you . . . no matter how angry, frustrated, self-
judgmental, fearful, lonely, sad, bitter, no matter how
betrayed you sometimes feel, I did not betray you. I
did not betray love, neither did life, and no matter
how caught up you get with life, I am glad. Let it take
you. Let yourself feel it. I am there . . . wherever you
are and whenever you let yourself feel, there is no risk,
no real danger of separation, remember this."

"I hear you, and sometimes you all need to
know . . ."

Jason is now talking to the entire chat room . . .

". . . that it's more than signs, and more than
making a light flicker, more than proving ourselves
. . . you can't feel me until you first feel this. There

is a reason you question the afterlife . . . how could you question its existence if you did not know somewhere deep inside your soul that it is real . . . I am real . . . what part of you is not real? And how do you know you are real? You feel it. You see the evidence of your existence . . . to see me is to see with new eyes, beyond vision. . . ."

And now he's talking to me again.

". . . you gave my spirit an ability to express in life . . . but I was real even before the form . . . love you Mom . . . have your cake . . . eat it, too."

The next section is a definite message to everyone. I do not remember anything specific that triggered such a "lesson" but am sure that someone in the chat room was needing to hear it, if not all of us.

Cyntha typed, "You have to believe, before you can receive the evidence you want. If you approach us with a limit to your belief, then we can only reach you with limitation, we can only connect to you from your soul/spirit/heart, and if your heart has limits, then so does the communication . . . sometimes you want us to 'prove' ourselves to you, but you never asked that of us in life. You never said, 'Prove to me you are real, Jason' when I was living there, so why now? I know you believe in this, but still sometimes believe it happens outside of you, but this communication can't happen unless it first reaches inside you. You first feel it, then you 'know' it. It's okay to be skeptical, but remember, to doubt spirit is to doubt your own true self and this communion takes place only according to what you believe *can* occur. Otherwise, you won't perceive it . . . we meet you from within and that connection manifests from that point . . . expect miracles."

There is one other reading with Cyntha that I want to explain. It took place in late August and the only thing I actually recall clearly is that Cyntha saw Jason take something out of his pocket. It went something like this:

"Does Dave have a hologram?" she asked.

"No, not that I can think of. Why?"

"Jason has one in his pocket. He took it out and said something about his dad. Let me see what else he says."

"Okay."

"Oh. He says he is *going* to give it to his dad. It looks round, and about the size of a quarter."

So I told Dave to watch for one. About two weeks later, we were on our way home from work, and out of the blue I mentioned the hologram. Dave said he thought he had one somewhere. I shook my head and said (for no reason that I was consciously aware of), "No. You haven't got it yet. You need to watch for one. It will be a new one, from Jason."

Later that same evening, Dave opened a box of Cracker Jacks. He held it out to me and asked me to open the surprise. I dug around in the box, pulled out the little white package, and ripped it open. A hologram, round, size of a quarter.

Now I know that Jason didn't put that hologram in that box. But I do believe he was able to look ahead (remember, no time in his world) and see

Dave opening that box with that prize in it. Then he simply turned it into a gift from him by telling Cyntha it was going to happen.

It was rocketing.

Mom has a hard time when I am philosophizing. To her, I still wear smelly socks and throw my clothes all over the floor. Talking to Ocallah, with her belief system and consequent filters, was like spiritual karaoke. I mean I could give her the concept and it came out sounding like it was coming from a master guide. Made me feel pretty "up there," let me tell you.

It's fun going to O cuz she knows me well enough to feel comfortable saying whatever she "hears." Even if it's Rayovac. Different mediums interpret different ways. It's a learning experience for all of us. Kind of trial and error.

One thing that keeps being sent from here to there, consistently over and over, is gratitude. Gratitude from spirit to loved ones for being open to our messages and not closing the door in fear. So much healing can happen when we are allowed to touch you and share the light. But we are not able to do that unless you believe it can happen. Mom knows it can happen, and when she didn't know it, she was determined to make it so it could. Remember . . . expect miracles.

15

Mediumship
Bits and Pieces

Purpose

There is not a moment
In your lifetime without meaning.
Each breath you take has purpose
and each soul you meet has come to you to receive a gift.
Never miss the opportunity to stop and rummage
  through your heart
for the treasure each soul seeks.
It is not yours to keep . . .
  in the beginning,
But once given,
it becomes yours.

— Sandy, 2000

EARLY THIS SUMMER, JASON CAME THROUGH WITH A MESSAGE via a medium I had met online. She informed me that Jason's friend with "a black truck . . . red trim . . . recently married . . . is going to be having a baby . . . and I see pink." Three months later, it was confirmed. I called the soon to be a mother and said, "I knew it before you did. Jason told me." (I am sure I was the subject at dinner that night.) Even though ultrasound has declared the child a male, the fact that Jason knew at or before conception is incredible.

When Jeremy's puppy (small and brown) was killed this fall, he called to tell me he had "sent" him to Jason. Less than a week had gone by when I was private-messaged by Caroline, another online medium. She asked me if Jason had a puppy. I asked why, and she said, "He is showing himself and a small brown puppy. The puppy is jumping all over him, licking and kissing, and Jason is hugging and loving him back."

During a reading in late 1997, a medium from Erie, Pennsylvania, delivered a message from James Michael, a baby boy we had lost (stillbirth) in 1976. The information firmly validated who was coming through. However, at the end of the communication from this infant I had really never known, Natalie clearly heard, "Tell John . . . hello." Only Jason would say that. It is my belief that this was Jason's way of letting me know that he, and James Michael, were one and the same.

Three different mediums have at three different times told me that when they see Jason he is "hovering" (always the risk taker). He has mentioned "the book" or "writing" in half a dozen messages.

My mom has come through with Jason and with my brother. Both times she made a big deal about her purse. In one she said, "See, you *can* take it with you." After Mom's funeral, I found a few bills tucked in her drawer under the shelf lining. Her own stash of mad money, I am sure.

My brother, Gary, has appeared several times. He spoke warmly of his two daughters, presented his

Harley emblem, a ring he had created and wore, and a wheelchair (he was paraplegic). The wheelchair came after he couldn't get Cyntha to understand his "walking like a robot," which is what Gary did when he was wearing his leg braces. He showed this same scene to a medium on the same day I typed this passage, only with my mom assisting him as he took "baby steps" with stiff legs. Gary also showed Cyntha a scene with him racing up and down halls in the wheelchair, zipping here and there. The chair he had ordered just before he passed was a chair designed specifically for speed.

There is no longer any reason for anyone who wants a reading with a medium not to have one. The problems of expense and distance no longer exist with the advent of the Internet. Most of the mediums who do online readings are "developing," and offer their abilities free of charge. Developing means they are just now discovering their gifts or are just "coming out" after years of hiding what they thought was too weird for most people to understand.

Old adages about spiritualism being the work of Satan or communication with our dead loved ones "holding them back" are simply nonsense. Fear was created to control the masses. It's time we left it behind us. Remember that anyone can claim to be a medium. It may take many readings before you find the one that feels right in your heart. But . . . once you find it and your heart feels like it's going to explode with joy, be sure and share the message with those who seem ready to hear it. We have gone long enough thinking that death created a wall between us and them. There is no wall. Only a door, standing open, surrounded by the light of love. Enter gently and you will be amazed at what you find.

Again, I just want to reiterate that it is not only okay, but is appreciated, when you talk to us. When we die and come back over to this side (which really isn't a side, but for lack of a better description . . .) we don't automatically become all knowing. We, well most of us that I know, still have much to experience and absorb. If we don't remember or haven't yet experienced the abilities of mediums and the power of our own energy (and by "our," I mean us over here and you over there), we may not make an attempt to contact you without your appeals for communication.

Also again, we aren't "too busy" to come to you. You can't hold us back. You have free will there; we have it here. And besides, even if we are busy, we can be in more than one place doing more than one thing, at the same . . . well . . . at your same time. Call us, visit your mediums, lose the fear. It's all okay as long as you follow your heart and act from love. . . .

16
Direct Contact

Searching

Closing my eyes, I search for you.
I breathe in the light of love
and release the tensions of this physical existence.
I reach with my mind to the spirit land,
while you watch with an amused smile.
Groping thru the fog and clutter, I feel for the physical
warmth of you . . .
And "see" you laugh.
"Mom," you say, "you can't feel love with your hand.
*   You have to feel it with your heart."*
Okay, I think. I can do that . . .
And once again I breathe . . . in with love . . . out with
*   the physical . . .*
in with love . . . out with the physical.
"MOM!! Stop trying so hard. Just listen. . . ."
My reply to him pounds in my head-
"I AM TRYING! I want so much to hear you. I miss
*   your laugh, your smile. It has been so long. . . ."*
In with love . . . out with the physical . . . In with love . . .
*   out with the physical . . .*
"Mom . . . I'm here."
I feel his smile . . . I hear him laugh . . .
"Who did you THINK you were talking to?"

Silence . . .
Warmth fills my heart as an unanticipated smile
   touches my lips.
My mind sends the words-
"Well . . . I THOUGHT I was talking to a part of myself. . . ."
and a soft whisper replies—
"and who more than your son is a part of you?"
Breathe . . . in with love . . . out with the physical . . .
   in with love . . . out with the physical . . .

— Sandy, 1999

I MADE MY FIRST UNASSISTED, *INITIATED-BY-ME* CONTACT with Jason during the first spring *after.* I had read about a method of connecting with those who have passed in a book by Bruce Moen called *Voyages into the Unknown.* It simply involves envisioning the person you wish to communicate with and remembering a conversation you had with them before they passed, where you were at, what both of you were wearing, etc. Once you have them firmly in mind (and heart), begin and maintain a dialogue with them "in your head." Imagine both sides of the conversation. Eventually, you will "imagine" a conversation that produces an answer or statement from the person who has died that you immediately know is not your imagination.

I had been practicing this technique for a month or two when I "pretended" asking Jason, "Will you still be there when I get there?" It is a universal fear of bereaved parents who are exploring nontraditional beliefs that our children might reincarnate and cease to exist on the other side. Since reuniting with them is our only saving grace, this is an intense fear that creates all kinds of problems. After questioning Jason, I immediately "saw" him roll his eyes (as in "how stupid can you be?") and answer, "Where else would I be? I was here even when I was there with you." Now, at the time, all I could think was *where did that come from and what the hell is that supposed to mean?* But now, after delving into the possibilities, I think I understand what he meant. I no longer fear my son not being there to meet me when I arrive.

Standing in front of the mirror one morning, curling my hair, I initiated one of our make-believe conversations. I cannot remember exactly what the subject was at the onset, but I know that it ended with Jason saying that each of us is here to experience different situations that result in growth for our soul. He went on to tell me, in our imaginary conversation, that Dave is here to experience survival, that I am here to feel what I am feeling with Jason's death, that Jeremy is here to learn serenity, and that Josh is here to master independence.

"Okay . . . so what was it you were here for and for such a short time?" I asked.

"To be loved."

Ready to read this book through and decide if it's good or a jumbled mess of words having little meaning to anyone but me, I told Jason I wanted him to "read along with me."

"Mom, I have read the book every single time you have sat down with it at the computer."

"Oh. Well, I didn't feel you there every time. . . ."

"That's your problem, not mine."

Lying on my bed, pondering life. I closed my eyes and found Jason. I remembered tickling his back to help him relax.

I wish I could tickle your back again, Jazz, I thought.

"You are. Right now." I imagined him saying.

"I mean I wish I could feel it."

"You are feeling it. You feel it spiritually, and pretty intensely, I would say."

"I *meeeeeeean* (I was getting frustrated) I wish I could *physically feel* tickling your back again."

"Why? When you did it physically, you didn't feel it like this. . . ."

I did help just a bit with this (grin). I wish that there was a gentler way for death to happen. Unfortunately, no one asked me for help when the whole thing started. At least not this part of me. As long as those in the physical refuse to look at death and invite her for dinner and spend some time getting to know her, this is the way it's going to be. There will come a time when it doesn't have to be this way but that time is not now.

I often hear folks asking mediums, "Is he all right now? Is he sad? Does he miss us?" I would like to answer.

Yes, we are all right now. When we left our bodies, we left our physical ailments. When we left our egos, we left our anger, our guilt, our shame, and our blame.

We aren't sad. Sad is for those of you who feel helpless, who can't seem to fix what is wrong. And there lies the problem. From our vantage point, nothing is wrong. From where we are, we can see each tiny piece of the puzzle and how one piece fits perfectly into the next one. We know that nothing is wrong.

And finally, no, we don't miss you. How can we miss someone that we are able to be with simply by thinking of them? We have no limits of time and space as you do. We hear every thought that you send out to us. We can be with you before you finish the thought. We are not gone. We are more with you now than we were before.

I want you to know that Mom has moved mountains to get to where she is now. It's been a long and most difficult trip, and she's not finished yet. I want you to know that she has realized that what she is looking for, the thing that she seeks, is not at the end of the journey but is the journey itself. She has never been so involved with life as she is now. There are those who say that believing in an afterlife creates a disregard for life before death. I beg to differ. Over and out.

17

Perks

Defenses

You come to me through a half open door.
I see you approach and wonder what you want.
Coveting my treasures,
I hide them from view,
Fearing your needs.
I see the you that is physically here but forget the
*   soul that holds you.*
I hear your cries and cover my ears.
I see your terror and cover my eyes.
I feel your pain . . . and touch your soul.
I have forgotten too many times
That each soul I meet
Is my soul
That each spirit I touch
Is my spirit
We are one, you and I.
There is a gift for me hidden in your heart
And it is up to me
To reach in
And claim it.

— Sandy, 2000

A<small>S I'VE GONE FROM ZERO POINT TO WHEREVER THE HECK</small> it is I am now, "things" have come into my life. These are things that if they had happened to me *before* . . . I would either have not "seen" them, or would have sought help from a mental health professional.

The first thing I noticed is a heightened sense of intuition. I used to spend days making a decision. Gather the facts, ponder the consequences, worry over the possible pitfalls, freak out with friends and family, then forget it. Always play safe. Now . . . I feel. I spend some time alone, give the choice to whoever it is that hears me when I am talking to myself and when I am consciously *being* who I really am, I surrender to the universe. Whatever will be, will be. Sound scary? Yes. Does it work? Yes.

An illustration: I was feeling overworked, stressed, and burnt out at work. Dave and I had worked (and lived) at a residential group home with troubled adolescents for nearly fourteen years. I was seriously considering throwing in the towel on my personal goal of "making a difference for kids." After months of feeling tired and tense every time I returned to the job after time off, I finally stopped moaning long enough to ask myself, "Is this who I really am?" The answer was a resounding "No." I am not a stressed-out, tired, cranky—okay, saying another swear word here—bitch. That is not who I am. So I sat down that afternoon and asked the universe to take the problem and give me an answer I could understand. During the next week, I had two dreams. In the first one, I had quit my current job and taken one in another location but was still working with adolescents. As I arrived at work my first day, I found the "group home" I had been hired to work in was actually a large institution owned by a public agency. Before moving to Wyoming, I had worked in a nearly identical environment and despised it. I could feel the same heavy energy permeating my soul in the dream; the gossip, the politics, and the "we're here to make money, not make a difference" kind of attitude. The dream was close to a nightmare.

The very next night, I had another dream. I had taken a position as an administrative assistant, something I think I could do and enjoy, in a small town in Florida, definitely a change from Wyoming. I arrived at work and met with the female administrator I would be assisting, a very congenial, stylish individual. Within an hour of starting my first day's work, I was cooking in a kitchen that had to be 120 degrees and wondering how I was going to have time to scrub the floor before serving the meal. My administrator had disappeared. The message was clear in both of these dreams. All jobs have their down side, and the grass is *not* always greener. . . .

Slowing down and asking for assistance, whether it be for a major life shift or locating the car keys is not only effective, it's soothing. The simple act of stopping to ask slows me down long enough to *feel what I am being,* rather than losing myself in what I am *doing.*

Somewhere along the road I became interested in out-of-body experiences. I read a few books and knew some of the beginning stages. As I lay in bed one night trying to meditate without falling asleep, I felt my body begin to shake. It felt like someone had started a jackhammer by my side of the bed. There was no sound, no pain or discomfort, and no movement when I opened my eyes to look at my body to see if it was bouncing all over the bed. As soon as my eyes focused on my body, the vibration stopped. I did have a fleeting thought of *"Oh, my God, I think I could be dying!"* which I would imagine was another reason I stayed in my body that night. It happened again twice, at approximately three month intervals. I know it is a "pre-OBE" for me, but I have no clue why I have never gotten past that stage.

John Edward has mentioned flying when he was younger, which were undoubtedly out-of-body "flights" unrecognized. On the night that our family heard John talk about this on a television special, Joshua spoke up and told us that he and Jason had "flown" all over the house many nights when they were between ten and twelve years old. Dave verified that they had told him about it at the time. But that was *before*. We weren't listening.

There was a period of about six months last spring when I experienced some very intense dreams. I cannot put a label on what they were or why they happened. The best I can do is give you my opinion, but first let me share the dreams.

Dream #1: I woke up hearing "Alaskan Airlines." Two hours later, my boss asked me if I'd heard about Alaskan Airlines and the crash that occurred during the night, killing over a hundred people.

Dream #2: I dreamed about a group counseling session with our boys at the group home. One of them was terribly upset because his hamster had been missing from its cage and he had just found it that evening. (Sorry, graphic violence coming up.) He was dead, and someone had stabbed the hamster in the eye with a pencil.

Two days later, I learned from a friend that a woman from our area had been attacked by a man who stabbed her in the eyes with a screwdriver. The vicious attack had occurred the same night as my dream.

Dream #3: I had two puppies that I left in a gymnasium overnight. When I went back to get them, they weren't there. I later saw them running through some bushes and undergrowth, but they were losing their hair. The next time I saw them, they were dead, floating in a small pool of water. They were identical puppies, and they were totally without hair when they died. They reminded me of baby hamsters or mice, all pink skin, and eyes not yet open.

I began a news search on the Internet for twins and drowned. I located what I believe is a connection. On the same night as my dream, a coed in a university several states away had given birth to twin fetuses. They had been found in the toilet in a dormitory rest room. They were premature and would not have lived even if they had been born in a hospital.

The only explanation I can come up with for these strange synchronistic events is that my energy somehow crossed over into the intense energy generated by the fear of the people involved. It's as if while sleeping, my energy (spirit, soul, inner self, etc.) was out and about, which I believe happens to all of us every time we let go enough to enter the sleep state. While wandering around out there, it ran across the intense energy of those events. For some odd reason, I then remembered it when I woke up.

Recently, as I fall asleep at night or enter a meditative state, I have started seeing faces. Faces of people I have never met, and faces of people who look oddly familiar but are out of my memory's reach. This has progressed from faces looking like photographs, no movement, no feeling, to the present faces being animated. There is still no sound or feeling to interpret, but I feel sure that the next few months will offer me that challenge.

Jason has informed me in several readings that he is doing the same thing there that we do here. That there is a link. He told John Edward that he is "meeting the same people." I assumed he was referring to those who have passed that "belong to" people that I have met. After a few experiences this summer and early fall, I have altered that assumption.

During the first year and a half after Jason's death, another bereaved mom whom had become an incredible friend, built a Website for Jason. Thank you, Cheryl. As I became more proficient on the computer, I expanded and updated Jason's Page. It is not a memorial site, though some would call it that, but is a celebration of his life, both before and after his death. One evening, when entering a chat room, a woman thanked me for "lending" her Jason. When I asked her what she meant, she explained that she had visited his site the night before. She had been despondent over her daughter's death and had connected with Jason as she read about his life. She told me that she spent the night conversing with my son, and that he had comforted her and gave her peace.

Less than a month later, I received two e-mails from members of a mailing list whose topic is *Crossing Over with John Edward* on the SciFi channel. Both had stories to tell about connecting with Jason. Both gave me chills, a sure sign for me of their authenticity. As I sat outside the health club where I work out waiting for a friend to arrive, I pondered the three recent connections made to my son, basically by total strangers. All three had been to Jason's Website. Besides these three acknowledgments of actual conversations with Jason, many others have commented on feeling Jason's energy when they visited his site.

So . . . I asked him. "Jason, tell me if I'm on the right track here. Are you connecting directly with people still here?" And since he so often nudges me to turn the radio on at the right moment, or to change a channel, or actually changes it himself, I asked him to answer me with a song. I waited for the nudge, got it, turned on the radio, and . . . *"Ohhhhhhh . . . I've got friends in **low** places. . . ."*

All I want to say here is that energy is constantly changing and moving. Thoughts create reality. If you are reading our story on a Web page, or talking to us in your head, or remembering a time you spent with us, you are calling us to you. Nine times out of ten, we're ready to answer. Whether you hear us or not is up to you.

18
Where Am I Now?

One

Falling into the void
of eternity
Waves of emotion
Flood my senses
Searching for you
Reaching out . . . touching what I think is you
but finding me.
Realizing
that I am you
and you are me
and all is one and the same
here in the center of our soul.

— Sandy, 2000

As I type this line, it has been 1,507 days, three hours, and 50 minutes since I last saw Jason saunter up our street to his death. Not a day has gone by without him being my first thought in the morning and my final one before drifting off to sleep. It is impossible to define the impact his life (both before and after dying) has had on my existence. Words alone do not do justice to such experiences. There must be feelings. I do not know that I am writer enough to put the feelings inside of the words. Perhaps Jason will help me.

I miss him. I ache for him, I cry for him, I reach for him. He is my child. I gave him my heart when I first looked into his eyes 22 years ago. He reached in and pulled it out with his tiny little fist, and when he left his material existence, he took the energy of that heart with him, still clutched in his hand. We are forever linked. Love does not disappear because an electrical line destroys the body's ability to function. Such a possibility almost seems ludicrous. I have no doubt about my son's existence in another level of reality, or of our connection being eternal.

My "ideas" seem to mushroom on a daily basis. They come to me through books, through the words of friends, through meditation, and through dreams. They sometimes sneak in and are in place before I even recognize them, while others enter with the blare of trumpets and blinding light. I could write another book about what I think happens when we die and why I think it happens that way, but it would only be my book of my ideas. Your book, your truth, is in your heart, not on these pages. It is enough to say that I have found, or perhaps remembered, a faith that comforts me when missing Jason threatens to obscure loving him.

Sometimes in the middle of the night, I lie awake and stare at the empty place beside my bed. I beg Jason to come, to "show up" and say "'night, Mom" just one more time. Once he told me that he could appear anytime he wanted to. He said that I am the obstacle. "You will not be able to 'see' me until you are capable of acknowledging it as a gift rather than perceiving it as another loss when I'm unable to stay." My intent is to become capable of that.

Do I still hurt? Yes. I hurt when I hear a mother scream at her child to shut up and leave her alone. I hurt because it took a catastrophic loss to propel me out of apathy and onto the path. I grieve because I could have spent my time with Jason talking about love and feelings and laughter instead of how messy his bedroom was or how he needed to find a job. I hurt because I said, "You'll have to wait, I am *working* right now" too often and too willingly. I hurt because I have so much wonder inside of me that can only seep out at convenient moments with specific individuals. I ache because while I know my son lives, many others believe he is gone. I hurt because I cannot say to my colleagues over lunch, "I talked to Jason last night. He's fine and we had a good talk." I hurt for those who have so much fear mixed in with their spirituality they can't get close enough to touch the love. And I hurt because many of us are so afraid of death we are incapable of living.

I hurt because right now, at this moment, there's a mom out there somewhere, sitting at a table with a cold cup of coffee. She's feeling like she can't breathe and hoping she won't. Detached from the activity around her, she sits in silence and watches the hands on the clock . . . tick . . . tick . . . tick . . . In just a few hours she will go to the mortuary to tell her child good-bye. I hurt because no one is going to tell her that good-bye isn't necessary and because even if someone did, she still has to find the meaning of that on her own, in her own time.

Mom hurts because one of the hardest lessons we have to learn in the physical is that although we do have to feel the pain, we do not have to classify that feeling as negative. At least not eternally. Death is no different than birth, except that when we "die" on this side, everyone sees us off and wishes us goodwill. You can do the same on your side when you remember who you are, and why. Remembering who you are, who we all are, makes death nothing more than a change in form. The absence you experience of souls who move on is simply an illusion.

19
In the Beginning

Candle

The night is cold and the air still
Lights blink rhythmically in our front yard.
I watch the clock click through the numbers . . . 7:55 . . . :56 . . .
I close my eyes and find you there; candle in one hand,
   a child's shoulder in the other,
Silly grin on your face, no different than before.
You do your little dance and pose for my "camera" . . . :57 . . .
Suddenly, I feel your joy, the peace you carry with you,
   and the warmth of your light.
Chills ripple down my spine and tears flood my still closed eyes.
It comes to me (from you? from me?) that lighting this
   candle is not in your "memory."
It is not a replacement for your presence.
You are HERE.
My candle is lit in gratitude . . . :58 . . .
Your life goes on, as does mine,
And in all sincerity,
My participation in your life now, and in my own,
Is more RIGHT than it ever was before . . . :59 . . . 7:00 p.m.
It is time.
I strike the match, reach for my candle, and . . .
You smile.
Your candle, a torch held high in celebration,
glows with the brilliance of eternal life.

— Sandy, 1999

I T SEEMS APPROPRIATE TO END THIS BOOK WITH ITS beginning.

In June of this year, Dave and I traveled to Salt Lake City, Utah, to see John Edward in person. Although John and I had e-mailed sporadically for over three years, we had never physically met. We drove down to Utah, about a six-hour trip, unpacked in a rather dumpy hotel room, and arrived at the Salt Palace where John was presenting. The room was about half full when we got our tickets, and we reserved our seats with my purse and a piece of paper that looked official and wasn't. Dave took our gift of gaily wrapped orange slice candy up to the table that was set up on the stage and placed it by what we hoped was John's water.

Counting chairs, we estimated about 400 people in attendance. As the clock moved toward 2 P.M., I watched those entering, searching for a friend I had met on the Griefnet mailing list. Gigi, who's daughter Kelsey had passed a few days after Jason, arrived shortly after us and we settled in for the lecture. I continue to be amazed at the relationships formed online that are just as real as those we form with our neighbors and co-workers. And yet we continue, as a human race, to argue that what we cannot see is not there.

John was introduced by his promoter, and then by two local DJ's. He bounded onto the foot-high stage and mesmerized the audience from his first statement. After about 40 minutes of fascinating details and anecdotes about spirit and mediumship, he was ready to move on to readings.

". . . but before I begin passing on messages to you, I have something else to share. Today is kind of a special day because . . ."

My heart was immediately in my throat. John went on to reveal how Jason went to him that weekend in June of 1997. He talked about our e-mail correspondence before and after and explained that we had never actually met. He then asked Dave and me to identify ourselves by raising our hands, which we did. I have no idea how I got up from my seat, since by then I was an emotional wreck, but I suddenly found myself in front of the room, hugging the man who had made my son, and my life, real again. Heart still in my throat, I returned to my chair and collapsed.

You need to know that my mom would rather jump out of an airplane without a parachute than stand in front of any gathering involving more than three individuals. Her getting out of that chair was the first divinely orchestrated occurrence of the day. The second one was when she hugged John, because she also hugged me. I was right there. The circle was complete.

John then set about proving to the room that death is not an end. His ability is incredible, and his persistence in getting the message through is impeccable. Both tears and laughter were plentiful as he delivered one message after another to those who were in the right place at the right time in their life. The air was filled with energy, and I wouldn't have been surprised to see streaks of light shooting out between John and the individuals receiving messages.

As he began winding down to the end of the seminar, John asked for questions from the audience. While he was answering one from a man about ten rows in front of us, he stopped in the middle of a sentence and pointed at Dave and me.

"Your son is here."

Jason then gave John a notepad full of validating information, some of which had already happened, some of which happened in the next few weeks, and some that is happening as I write this chapter. It was tremendously empowering for us to actually be in the same room with John as he delivered Jason's message. The four of us were together in one spot, a situation I had known would occur from the very first time I saw JE as the signature on an e-mail.

John heard me loud and clear. He got it all right, and I especially liked the way I got his attention. He wasn't hearing me, or paying attention or something, maybe cuz he knows Mom and doesn't always feel comfortable reading for "friends." But anyway, I showed him a sign. With Mom's name on it. It was sort of like "Here's Your Sign," but it turned out okay, cuz Mom's name was on the sign in the window of a city bus that went right by the Salt Palace, and also on the interstate overpass, directing traffic to Sandy (Utah). I was impressed with myself.

Sometime during John's reading, he explained that he only hears a middle name when the first name is the same as someone else involved in the reading. For instance, during our reading, if a second Jason were to appear or Jason wanted to acknowledge another Jason, he might use their middle name to clarify. About a week after our reading in Salt Lake, a light came on. Actually, it flared.

To refresh your memory, during our June reading with John in '97, he mentioned a young man being with Jason. He said he was connected to a "D" and an Anna or Ann, and had suffered a self-inflicted gunshot. During John's next reading in August, he spoke extensively about Jason wanting us to know he had Chris with him. He said Chris had died from an impact, was male or female, was young, March was important, as was New Jersey. He also saw a Snoopy with erect ears during that reading.

During the joint reading with John and Shelley Peck, and in a reading with Natalie during the same period of time, Jason was with another Jason. John said they had something in common besides their names and also asked if I had dialogued with a mother who had a connection to New Jersey.

Shortly after I came out of *The Fog,* and began using the Internet to find other parents who had lost a child, I met a woman from the other side of Wyoming who had also lost a child. Susie's son, Jason, was obviously the other Jason mentioned in John and Shelley's reading and in Natalies. What wasn't so obvious was the fact that "the other Jason" . . . was also the mysterious Chris.

Susie's son's middle name was Christopher. He passed in March of 1997, had lived in Jersey for a short period, had died of an accidental self-inflicted gunshot, and had a relative by the name of Ann or Anna. Jason Christopher and my Jason both lived in Wyoming, both had the same first name, and both were born on the fifth of a month.

Only the Snoopy with erect ears remained unexplained but only until I asked Susie if she had a "Snoopy something" by or on her computer. In reply, I received an e-mail from her on stationery with a background of . . . yep, you guessed it . . . several Snoopys . . . with very erect ears. In the foreground was a Snoopy announcing, "*I shall return.*" Also of interest is the fact that Jason Christopher spent his last evening alive playing on Susie's computer.

Man, was I glad she finally "got" this one. I was really tired of my mom asking everyone and their dog if they had a Chris that had passed after me who was connected to March and New Jersey. I think everyone and their dog was tired of it, too.

After John's wrap-up, we stood in line for a book signing. I was running from inside to outside to inside again, and as I moved about the different attendees, people kept telling me, "I'm so-and-so in the chat room" or "I know Jason, this was so incredible." I was running on adrenaline and couldn't believe how many lives Jason had touched. I was also able to assist a newly bereaved mom in contacting a local Compassionate Friends chapter, which reminded me of the grieving that must occur before it is possible to reach the rooftop I was once again screaming from.

Even I felt amazed. I mean, I do "get around" a bit, but I had no idea that this many people would remember Jason from a chat room or Jason from John's book. It's a good thing I don't have that ego thing anymore.

I awoke the next morning with a feeling of heightened emotion. I swallowed tears all the way home, and I tried to explain to Dave what I didn't understand myself. Words fell short of describing what I was feeling. I only know that it was incredible and wondrous and intensely transformative. I continued to feel this throughout the week, and could not get through telling the story of our visit to see John Edward without crying. I talked to Jason constantly, asking for advice and clarity as to what was going on, but all I could see when I "turned to his channel" was that goofy grin of his that can only be interpreted as "Gotcha!"

Mom had to get this one herself. She was soooo ready to move on. But she had to find the reason inside. It was there. Every time she started crying and would say "What is this????" I would slap my hand over my mouth to make sure I didn't give it away. Thank God she's still a little rusty in the feeling energy department.

Finally at the end of the week, I was able to find Cyntha in the chat room. She asked about John and how it went, and of course I started to cry. However, one nice thing about chatting is you can still type while you're crying as long as you have tissues by the computer. I was able to share what took place in a way that made her understand the *hugeness* of our experience, and she validated what I was feeling. She talked about how powerful it must be to know that people who didn't know my son while he was alive, now know him and consider him a friend. She talked about how many people he and I have touched and how necessary it has all been. As I "listened" to her, she too began to cry, and I realized how important it was that I share what had transpired in Jason's life and afterlife.

As I pondered what the main message was for me in all that had happened, I typed (or Jason did), "I can't believe that there are mom's out there who think their kid is dead." Wham. Nothing like getting hit with a ton of V-8. That was it. I wanted to share. I knew then that it was time to tell our story.

I'd like to take the credit, but it wasn't me. It was Mom all the way, worked through it all and came up with her own experience. I might have let her know when she finally got it that she was right on and I think what she felt was a ton of V-8 was actually more like a psychic head butt.

I began pondering a book, I talked to Jason, and I prayed (again, to anyone and anything that might be listening) for insight. Was it possible? Could I write? Would anyone publish it? How would I find a market? I e-mailed John to see what he thought. He had written a book and knew what was required. Being the busy person that he is, he didn't respond. Days went by, no mention of the book idea. Did that mean it sucked? Did he even have time to read that e-mail?

Get in here, Jason!

"Jason," I said, "If you think this is such a good idea, then *you* need to get your buddy John on the phone to me or on the computer. I need a nudge in the right direction or I am going to assume this is a stupid idea and let it go." Two hours later, John e-mailed me. He encouraged me to go for it and I started typing.

The process has been magical. I can hardly wait to see what lies around the next corner. I hope that somewhere along this road, your path and mine will cross, and you will wave me over to rest under a huge shade tree. You will share your story with me, and after the tears, our laughter will ring through the valley, and even those in *The Pit* will smile at the magic. . . .

I hope you have been able to feel the words in this book. What Mom and I want, is to give you a reason to get up tomorrow morning. A reason to breathe. A reason to laugh again. We are not dead. We are as alive, if not more so, than we were before. We love, we laugh, we live. Believe in us, open your heart again, and we will show you . . . Love Never Leaves.

Afterword

Love Never Dies

There is no end
To anything;
No separation,
No division.
We have confused illusion with reality.
Instead see this.
An unbroken circle of light,
Expanding,
Intensifying,
Until the illusion of separation
  Ceases . . .
    To . . .
      Exist.

— Sandy, 2001

IN LATE NOVEMBER, I SET MY DEADLINE TO HAVE THE manuscript in the mail by December 15. I planned to spend the weekend of the eighth tying up loose strings and getting the book out of my reach. Jason and Joshua's birthday was the fifth. We went out for pizza and spent the evening with Josh and his fiancé. It was a nice evening, but also a "missing Jason" time for all of us.

The next evening, I plumped my pillows and settled into bed at the group home with a good book. I turned up the scanner (which alerted us to possible new arrivals) and before I had even found my bookmarked page, the scanner crackled to life.

". . . self-inflicted gunshot wound to the chest, 23-year-old male . . ." and our home address.

I was instantly propelled back in time to 1996. Once again, we quickly dressed and drove to the hospital. Once again, we arrived at the same time as the ambulance. Once again, a son was wheeled into the same unit and placed on the same gurney. I was trapped in a recurrent nightmare with no hope of awakening. I was paralyzed with fear. And then I remembered . . . *there are things that we can't control and things that we can.*

I walked into the hospital and firmly planted myself in the doorway to the trauma unit. *Look at me, Josh.* . . . No less than six medical personnel worked frantically in the room. Machines were beeping, instruments were clanging, and orders were shouted over the din. I held my ground. *Look at me, Josh . . . look at me.* Joshua's eyes met mine. I told him I loved him. I prayed for love. I prayed for strength.

Although it seemed like an eternity, we had been there less than 20 minutes when we were told that the injury to the upper lobe of Josh's right lung was not life threatening. The most pressing issue was an inadequate local supply of blood, and he was flown to Casper to alleviate that problem. After surgery the next morning, he began the healing process.

With my first huge sigh of relief, I began questioning my own distance from what was obviously a "should have seen this coming" incident. Why did Josh do this? Had I forgotten him while searching for Jason? Had I spent too much time missing Jason and not enough time loving Josh? I had tried so hard to balance the two sides of my life, the "Jason side" and the "everything else side." Why had this happened? What was I forgetting?

The answers came slowly, but they came. From the beginning, Josh assured us that he had no intention of killing himself. He simply needed the pain to stop. He had put off grieving his brother's death for four and a half years and had just spent his fifth birthday alone (a twin without a twin means alone, regardless of how many others are present.) With another loss breathing down his neck, and an imminent breakup with his fiancé, he elected to use a gun to tell the world he'd had enough.

Had I overlooked Josh and left him floundering for nearly five years? My heart tells me no. Josh had chosen his own path, as we all had, and had walked it at his own pace in his own direction. I believe we all have to reach that ground-zero point where we want to feel differently. No, neglecting Josh while focusing on Jason did not seem to be the essence of all of this. Then what was the lesson? What was I forgetting?

As I sat by Josh's hospital bed one night, watching him sleep, I decided to send him love as I had learned to do with Jason. Picturing him as he was at about four years of age, I picked him up and held him on my lap. *It's all okay, baby . . . you'll be fine . . . I love you. . . .* We rocked for a while and I wiped away his tears. *There . . . isn't that better. . . . You're okay now . . . aren't you? I love you. . . .* Just as I imagined the glimmer of a smile lighting up his little face, I felt the familiar whooooosh of love that Jason had introduced me to. The circle was complete . . . and suddenly I remembered . . .

. . . separation is an illusion. For four and a half years, I had tried to segregate that which is the same. I had built a wall between the spiritual and the physical, which in reality was as ludicrous as dividing the ocean with a piece of string. I had attempted to balance the time I spent doing and being, and often worried about slighting either the physical or the spiritual side of my life. I had categorized my life into before and after, but had forgotten the only time that really matters . . . is now.

Sitting with Josh that evening, I remembered that I didn't need to shut one door before opening another. I didn't need to leave here, to go there. I didn't need to go back, before moving forward. And I didn't need to leave Josh to be with Jason, or leave Jason to be with Josh. I only had to come from love and everything would flow together. It was time to step back into life.

Amen. . . .

Light for the Journey

Books

By John Edward

What If God Were the Sun?
2000, Jodere

Crossing Over: The Stories Behind the Stories
2001, Jodere

One Last Time: A Psychic Medium Speaks to Those We Have Loved and Lost
1998, Berkeley

By Joel Martin, Patricia Romanowski

Our Children Forever: George Anderson's Messages from Children on the Other Side
1994, Berkeley

Love Beyond Life: The Healing Power of After-Death Communications
1997, HarperCollins

By Joel Martin, George Anderson, Patricia Romanowski

We Don't Die: George Anderson's Conversations With the Other Side
1988, G.P. Putnam's Sons

By Bill Guggenheim, Judy Guggenheim

Hello from Heaven!
1996, Bantam

By George Anderson, Andrew Barone

George Anderson's Lessons from the Light: Extraordinary Messages of Comfort and Hope from the Other Side
1999, G.P. Putnam's Sons

By Suzane Northrop, Kate McLoughlin

Seance: Healing Messages from Beyond
1995, Dell

By Gordon Livingston M.D., Mark Helprin (Foreword)

Only Spring: On Mourning the Death of My Son
1999, HarperSanFrancisco

By Neale Donald Walsch

Conversations With God:
An Uncommon Dialogue (Book 1)
1996, G.P. Putnam's Sons
(also **Book 2** and **Book 3**, Hampton Roads, 1997 and 1998)

The Little Soul and the Sun: A Children's
Parable Adapted from Conversations With God
Frank Riccio (Illustrator)
Reading level: Ages 4–8
1998, Hampton Roads

Friendship With God: An Uncommon Dialogue
1999, G.P. Putnam's Sons

By Gary Zukav

The Seat of the Soul
1989, Simon & Schuster

Soul Stories
2000, Simon & Schuster

By Bruce Moen

Voyages into the Unknown
(Exploring the Afterlife Series, Vol. 1)
1997, Hampton Roads
(also **Vol. 2, 3,** and **4**)

By James Van Praagh

Talking to Heaven:
A Medium's Message of Life After Death
1999, Dutton

Television Shows

Crossing Over with John Edward
(Check your local listings)

Internet Resources

—Mediumship—

http://www.ocallah.com

http://www.johnedward.net

http://www.spiritspace.net

http://www.georgeanderson.com

http://www.johnedwardfriends.org

http://groups.yahoo.com/group/CrossingOver

—Life After Death—

http://www.after-death.com

http://www.afterlife-knowledge.com

—Spirituality—

http://www.zukav.com

http://www.spiritweb.com

http://www.conversationswithgod.org

—Grief Support—

http://www.widownet.com

http://www.griefnet.org

http://www.compassionatefriends.org

http://www.griefhealing.com

http://www.beyondindigo.com

http://www.webhealing.com

About the Author

Four years after the death of her son Jason, Sandy Goodman realized she had found a way to survive the unthinkable. She sat down and began writing the story of her journey through grief, hoping to reach others who needed a light in the darkness. *Love Never Dies: A Mother's Journey from Loss to Love* is her first book.

Sandy is the founder, Chapter Leader, and Newsletter Editor of the Wind River Chapter of The Compassionate Friends. She and her husband Dave have been Resident Counselors in a group home for at-risk youth in central Wyoming for 15 years, and are both actively involved in the Wyoming Association for Child and Youth Care Professionals.

If you would like to contact Sandy, please visit her website at: **http://www.loveneverdies.net.**